THIS BOOK MAY BE RENEWED

The Department of Justice

The Department of Justice

Lynne Dunn

CHELSEA HOUSE PUBLISHERS

On the cover: Detail of C. Paul Jennewein's *Coat of Arms of the United States*, 1933–35. This inscription and seal appears at the attic level at the corners of Ninth and Tenth Streets on Pennsylvania Avenue.

Frontispiece: A February 2, 1933, photograph showing the Justice Building under construction.

Chelsea House Publishers
Editor-in-Chief: Nancy Toff
Executive Editor: Remmel T. Nunn
Managing Editor: Karyn Gullen Browne
Copy Chief: Juliann Barbato
Picture Editor: Adrian G. Allen
Art Director: Maria Epes
Manufacturing Manager: Gerald Levine

Know Your Government
Senior Editor: Kathy Kuhtz

Staff for THE DEPARTMENT OF JUSTICE
Copy Editor: Lisa Fenev
Deputy Copy Chief: Nicole Bowen
Editorial Assistant: Elizabeth Nix
Picture Coordinator: Melanie Sanford
Picture Research: Dixon & Turner Research Associates, Inc.
Assistant Art Director: Loraine Machlin
Senior Designer: Noreen M. Lamb
Production Coordinator: Joseph Romano

First Printing

1 3 5 7 9 8 6 4 2

Library of Congress Cataloging-in-Publication Data

Dunn, Lynne
    The Department of Justice / Lynne Dunn.
       p.   cm.—(Know your government)
    Bibliography: p.
    Includes index.
    Summary: Surveys the history of the Department of Justice and describes its structure, current function, and influence on United States society.
    ISBN 0–87754–843–9
         0–7910–0888–6 (pbk.)
    1. United States. Dept. of Justice—Juvenile literature.
[1. United States. Dept. of Justice.] I. Title. II. Series: Know your government
(New York, N.Y.)   89–72303
KF5107.D86 1989   CIP
353.5–dc20   AC

CONTENTS

KNOW YOUR GOVERNMENT

CHELSEA HOUSE PUBLISHERS

INTRODUCTION

Government: Crises of Confidence

Arthur M. Schlesinger, jr.

From the start, Americans have regarded their government with a mixture of reliance and mistrust. The men who founded the republic did not doubt the indispensability of government. "If men were angels," observed the 51st Federalist Paper, "no government would be necessary." But men are not angels. Because human beings are subject to wicked as well as to noble impulses, government was deemed essential to assure freedom and order.

At the same time, the American revolutionaries knew that government could also become a source of injury and oppression. The men who gathered in Philadelphia in 1787 to write the Constitution therefore had two purposes in mind. They wanted to establish a strong central authority and to limit that central authority's capacity to abuse its power.

To prevent the abuse of power, the Founding Fathers wrote two basic principles into the new Constitution. The principle of federalism divided power between the state governments and the central authority. The principle of the separation of powers subdivided the central authority itself into three branches—the executive, the legislative, and the judiciary—so that "each may be a check on the other." The *Know Your Government* series focuses on the major executive departments and agencies in these branches of the federal government.

The Constitution did not plan the executive branch in any detail. After vesting the executive power in the president, it assumed the existence of "executive departments" without specifying what these departments should be. Congress began defining their functions in 1789 by creating the Departments of State, Treasury, and War. The secretaries in charge of these departments made up President Washington's first cabinet. Congress also provided for a legal officer, and President Washington soon invited the attorney general, as he was called, to attend cabinet meetings. As need required, Congress created more executive departments.

Setting up the cabinet was only the first step in organizing the American state. With almost no guidance from the Constitution, President Washington, seconded by Alexander Hamilton, his brilliant secretary of the treasury, equipped the infant republic with a working administrative structure. The Federalists believed in both executive energy and executive accountability and set high standards for public appointments. The Jeffersonian opposition had less faith in strong government and preferred local government to the central authority. But when Jefferson himself became president in 1801, although he set out to change the direction of policy, he found no reason to alter the framework the Federalists had erected.

By 1801 there were about 3,000 federal civilian employees in a nation of a little more than 5 million people. Growth in territory and population steadily enlarged national responsibilities. Thirty years later, when Jackson was president, there were more than 11,000 government workers in a nation of 13 million. The federal establishment was increasing at a faster rate than the population.

Jackson's presidency brought significant changes in the federal service. He believed that the executive branch contained too many officials who saw their jobs as "species of property" and as "a means of promoting individual interest." Against the idea of a permanent service based on life tenure, Jackson argued for the periodic redistribution of federal offices, contending that this was the democratic way and that official duties could be made "so plain and simple that men of intelligence may readily qualify themselves for their performance." He called this policy rotation-in-office. His opponents called it the spoils system.

In fact, partisan legend exaggerated the extent of Jackson's removals. More than 80 percent of federal officeholders retained their jobs. Jackson discharged no larger a proportion of government workers than Jefferson had done a generation earlier. But the rise in these years of mass political parties gave federal patronage new importance as a means of building the party and of rewarding activists. Jackson's successors were less restrained in the distribu-

tion of spoils. As the federal establishment grew—to nearly 40,000 by 1861—
the politicization of the public service excited increasing concern.

After the Civil War the spoils system became a major political issue.
High-minded men condemned it as the root of all political evil. The spoilsmen,
said the British commentator James Bryce, "have distorted and depraved the
mechanism of politics." Patronage, by giving jobs to unqualified, incompetent,
and dishonest persons, lowered the standards of public service and nourished
corrupt political machines. Office-seekers pursued presidents and cabinet
secretaries without mercy. "Patronage," said Ulysses S. Grant after his
presidency, "is the bane of the presidential office." "Every time I appoint
someone to office," said another political leader, "I make a hundred enemies
and one ingrate." George William Curtis, the president of the National Civil
Service Reform League, summed up the indictment. He said,

> The theory which perverts public trusts into party spoils, making public
> employment dependent upon personal favor and not on proved merit,
> necessarily ruins the self-respect of public employees, destroys the
> function of party in a republic, prostitutes elections into a desperate
> strife for personal profit, and degrades the national character by lower-
> ing the moral tone and standard of the country.

The object of civil service reform was to promote efficiency and honesty in
the public service and to bring about the ethical regeneration of public life. Over
bitter opposition from politicians, the reformers in 1883 passed the Pendleton
Act, establishing a bipartisan Civil Service Commission, competitive examinations, and appointment on merit. The Pendleton Act also gave the president
authority to extend by executive order the number of "classified" jobs—that is,
jobs subject to the merit system. The act applied initially only to about 14,000
of the more than 100,000 federal positions. But by the end of the 19th century
40 percent of federal jobs had moved into the classified category.

Civil service reform was in part a response to the growing complexity of
American life. As society grew more organized and problems more technical,
official duties were no longer so plain and simple that any person of intelligence
could perform them. In public service, as in other areas, the all-round man was
yielding ground to the expert, the amateur to the professional. The excesses
of the spoils system thus provoked the counter-ideal of scientific public administration, separate from politics and, as far as possible, insulated against it.

The cult of the expert, however, had its own excesses. The idea that
administration could be divorced from policy was an illusion. And in the realm
of policy, the expert, however much segregated from partisan politics, can

9

never attain perfect objectivity. He remains the prisoner of his own set of values. It is these values rather than technical expertise that determine fundamental judgments of public policy. To turn over such judgments to experts, moreover, would be to abandon democracy itself; for in a democracy final decisions must be made by the people and their elected representatives. "The business of the expert," the British political scientist Harold Laski rightly said, "is to be on tap and not on top."

Politics, however, were deeply ingrained in American folkways. This meant intermittent tension between the presidential government, elected every four years by the people, and the permanent government, which saw presidents come and go while it went on forever. Sometimes the permanent government knew better than its political masters; sometimes it opposed or sabotaged valuable new initiatives. In the end a strong president with effective cabinet secretaries could make the permanent government responsive to presidential purpose, but it was often an exasperating struggle.

The struggle within the executive branch was less important, however, than the growing impatience with bureaucracy in society as a whole. The 20th century saw a considerable expansion of the federal establishment. The Great Depression and the New Deal led the national government to take on a variety of new responsibilities. The New Deal extended the federal regulatory apparatus. By 1940, in a nation of 130 million people, the number of federal workers for the first time passed the 1 million mark. The Second World War brought federal civilian employment to 3.8 million in 1945. With peace, the federal establishment declined to around 2 million by 1950. Then growth resumed, reaching 2.8 million by the 1980s.

The New Deal years saw rising criticism of "big government" and "bureau-cracy." Businessmen resented federal regulation. Conservatives worried about the impact of paternalistic government on individual self-reliance, on community responsibility, and on economic and personal freedom. The nation in effect renewed the old debate between Hamilton and Jefferson in the early republic, although with an ironic exchange of positions. For the Hamiltonian constituency, the "rich and well-born," once the advocate of affirmative government, now condemned government intervention, while the Jeffersonian constituency, the plain people, once the advocate of a weak central government and of states' rights, now favored government intervention.

In the 1980s, with the presidency of Ronald Reagan, the debate has burst out with unusual intensity. According to conservatives, government interven-tion abridges liberty, stifles enterprise, and is inefficient, wasteful, and

10

arbitrary. It disturbs the harmony of the self-adjusting market and creates worse troubles than it solves. Get government off our backs, according to the popular cliché, and our problems will solve themselves. When government is necessary, let it be at the local level, close to the people. Above all, stop the inexorable growth of the federal government.

In fact, for all the talk about the "swollen" and "bloated" bureaucracy, the federal establishment has not been growing as inexorably as many Americans seem to believe. In 1949, it consisted of 2.1 million people. Thirty years later, while the country had grown by 70 million, the federal force had grown only by 750,000. Federal workers were a smaller percentage of the population in 1985 than they were in 1955—or in 1940. The federal establishment, in short, has not kept pace with population growth. Moreover, national defense and the postal service account for 60 percent of federal employment.

Why then the widespread idea about the remorseless growth of government? It is partly because in the 1960s the national government assumed new and intrusive functions: affirmative action in civil rights, environmental protection, safety and health in the workplace, community organization, legal aid to the poor. Although this enlargement of the federal regulatory role was accompanied by marked growth in the size of government on all levels, the expansion has taken place primarily in state and local government. Whereas the federal force increased by only 27 percent in the 30 years after 1950, the state and local government force increased by an astonishing 212 percent.

Despite the statistics, the conviction flourishes in some minds that the national government is a steadily growing behemoth swallowing up the liberties of the people. The foes of Washington prefer local government, feeling it is closer to the people and therefore allegedly more responsive to popular needs. Obviously there is a great deal to be said for settling local questions locally. But local government is characteristically the government of the locally powerful. Historically, the way the locally powerless have won their human and constitutional rights has often been through appeal to the national government. The national government has vindicated racial justice against local bigotry, defended the Bill of Rights against local vigilantism, and protected natural resources against local greed. It has civilized industry and secured the rights of labor organizations. Had the states' rights creed prevailed, there would perhaps still be slavery in the United States.

The national authority, far from diminishing the individual, has given most Americans more personal dignity and liberty than ever before. The individual freedoms destroyed by the increase in national authority have been in the main

11

the freedom to deny black Americans their rights as citizens; the freedom to put small children to work in mills and immigrants in sweatshops; the freedom to pay starvation wages, require barbarous working hours, and permit squalid working conditions; the freedom to deceive in the sale of goods and securities; the freedom to pollute the environment—all freedoms that, one supposes, a civilized nation can readily do without.

"Statements are made," said President John F. Kennedy in 1963, "labelling the Federal Government an outsider, an intruder, an adversary. . . . The United States Government is not a stranger or not an enemy. It is the people of fifty states joining in a national effort. . . . Only a great national effort by a great people working together can explore the mysteries of space, harvest the products at the bottom of the ocean, and mobilize the human, natural, and material resources of our lands."

So an old debate continues. However, Americans are of two minds. When pollsters ask large, spacious questions—Do you think government has become too involved in your lives? Do you think government should stop regulating business?—a sizable majority opposes big government. But when asked specific questions about the practical work of government—Do you favor social security? unemployment compensation? Medicare? health and safety standards in factories? environmental protection? government guarantee of jobs for everyone seeking employment? price and wage controls when inflation threatens?—a sizable majority approves of intervention.

In general, Americans do not want less government. What they want is more efficient government. They want government to do a better job. For a time in the 1970s, with Vietnam and Watergate, Americans lost confidence in the national government. In 1964, more than three-quarters of those polled had thought the national government could be trusted to do right most of the time. By 1980 only one-quarter was prepared to offer such trust. But by 1984 trust in the federal government to manage national affairs had climbed back to 45 percent.

Bureaucracy is a term of abuse. But it is impossible to run any large organization, whether public or private, without a bureaucracy's division of labor and hierarchy of authority. And we live in a world of large organizations. Without bureaucracy modern society would collapse. The problem is not to abolish bureaucracy, but to make it flexible, efficient, and capable of innovation.

Two hundred years after the drafting of the Constitution, Americans still regard government with a mixture of reliance and mistrust—a good combination. Mistrust is the best way to keep government reliable. Informed criticism

12

is the means of correcting governmental inefficiency, incompetence, and arbitrariness; that is, of best enabling government to play its essential role. For without government, we cannot attain the goals of the Founding Fathers. Without an understanding of government, we cannot have the informed criticism that makes government do the job right. It is the duty of every American citizen to know our government—which is what this series is all about.

Although a five-man committee (from left to right, Thomas Jefferson, John Adams, Benjamin Franklin, Roger Sherman, and Robert Livingston) was enlisted to draft the Declaration of Independence, Thomas Jefferson was the document's main author. The declaration was formally adopted by delegates of the 13 colonies on July 4, 1776.

ONE

The Justice Ideal

T homas Jefferson sat at the writing desk in his small second-floor room in Philadelphia in the summer of 1776. The Virginia lawyer had just been appointed to a five-man committee responsible for drafting an extremely important message to the British government. This document was to state that the 13 British colonies in North America were no longer subject to the rule of King George III: They were 13 free and independent states, which would unite to form a new nation.

The declaration that finally flowed from Jefferson's pen stated, "We hold these truths to be self-evident, that all men are created equal, that they are endowed by their Creator with certain inalienable Rights, that among these are Life, Liberty and the pursuit of Happiness." These political ideals did not originate with Thomas Jefferson; they were a product of the colonists' English heritage, growing from the tradition of British parliamentary government and common law (a system of law established by court decisions based upon custom and precedent). Yet Jefferson's words and phrases were eloquent, and the ideals they expressed launched the American Revolution. When the new nation emerged from the war in 1783, free of British rule, the ideals set forth in the Declaration of Independence continued to guide the country.

71586

In 1641, Thomas Howard (top center), 14th earl of Arundel and lord high steward of England during the reign of King Charles I, presides over the trial of Thomas Wentworth, the earl of Strafford (bottom center), who was accused of treason and later beheaded. Congress incorporated many English legal traditions as well as the title of attorney general when creating the Office of the Attorney General in 1789.

In 1787, when the 55 delegates to the Constitutional Convention met in Philadelphia to create a new government, they communicated many of these same ideals in their writing. The Constitution replaced the ineffectual Articles of Confederation (which had been drafted by Congress in 1777 and ratified by the states in 1781). The new document began, "We the People of the United States, in Order to form a more perfect Union, establish Justice, insure domestic Tranquility, provide for the common defence, promote the general Welfare, and secure the Blessings of Liberty to ourselves and our Posterity, do ordain and establish this Constitution for the United States of America."

Together, the Declaration of Independence and the Constitution remain the fundamental documents of the nation. These documents are critically important because they established the new nation's democratic ideals and structure of government, asserting that all people are created equal. Laws must be created to ensure that brute force does not control people's interactions. Only when laws, fairly administered, define the relationship between citizen and citizen and between all citizens and their government, can men and women enjoy justice, peace, order, and security. Indeed, as the English philosopher Thomas Hobbes wrote in his book *Leviathan* (1651), a society without laws would be a society in which life was "solitary, poore, nasty, brutish, and short."

Over the last 200 years, Americans have tried to protect and preserve these ideals within their government, even as their society has changed. They have seen the government grow and have supported the creation of numerous departments and agencies to serve the needs of the nation. These agencies have changed over time to reflect new concerns and priorities. Yet each remains in line with its original purpose and democratic rule.

Few federal agencies and departments are as long standing and as crucial to the preservation of American democratic ideals as the Office of the Attorney General and the Department of Justice. The Office of the Attorney General has

The 17th-century English political philosopher Thomas Hobbes set forth the idea of a social contract, an agreement under which a society submits to the absolute authority of a government in return for the security promised by such an arrangement.

its origins in the earliest days of the nation. Established by the Judiciary Act of 1789, the position took its name—attorney general—and official motto—*Qui pro domina justitia sequitur* (Who prosecutes on behalf of justice)—from a similar position within the British government. The use of the same title and motto reflects the nation's British heritage and the founders' respect for the tradition of English common law. Congress created the Office of the Attorney General in the earliest days of the nation, a priority that indicates the importance of law enforcement to the preservation of the democracy.

Under the terms of the Judiciary Act, the attorney general, an executive-branch official, would serve as the lawyer for the federal government. He would prosecute all cases brought before the Supreme Court and advise presidents and executive department heads on legal matters. As the young nation grew and its legal affairs became increasingly complex, the attorney general's responsibilities increased. By 1870 it became clear that the nation needed an entire department to handle its legal needs, and so Congress created the Department of Justice.

The evolution of the Department of Justice reflects important changes in our society. Over time, the department developed specialized divisions to deal with particular areas of concern. The formation of the Civil, Criminal, Land and Natural Resources, Antitrust, Tax, and Civil Rights divisions, the Immigration and Naturalization Service, and two special investigative agencies, the Federal Bureau of Investigation (FBI) and the Drug Enforcement Administration

The Justice Department seal features an eagle perched on the shield of the United States, bearing an olive branch (symbolizing peace) and arrows (symbolizing war), and the motto Qui pro domina justitia sequitur *(Who prosecutes on behalf of justice).*

President George Bush (right) talks with Attorney General Richard Thorn-burgh in March 1989. Although the attorney general's responsibilities have increased in scope since the office was created in 1789, the basic function of the office has remained the same.

(DEA), reflects new perceptions and needs and tells a great deal about the changing nature of American society.

Throughout the department's history, however, the basic role of the attorney general has remained constant: to serve as the senior lawyer for the nation, responsible for ensuring that the federal government does not exercise its power unfairly, inconsistently, or arbitrarily. He or she provides legal advice to the president and, when requested, to the executive department heads so that these officials may fulfill their responsibilities in accordance with the law. In both these roles—as attorney for the government and as legal adviser to the executive branch—the attorney general is responsible for protecting one of the most cherished ideals of Americans: that relationships between the federal government and the states, between different agencies within the federal government, and between the government and U.S. citizens are guided by rules grounded in law, not in force. The Office of the Attorney General and the Department of Justice were created to assure that the United States remains a nation governed by law so that justice may be served.

Edmund Randolph became the nation's first attorney general in 1790. A well-respected Virginia lawyer and one of the framers of the Constitution, Randolph was appointed to serve as the lawyer for the federal government.

TWO

Men Learned in
the Law

When the representatives of the first Congress of the United States met on March 4, 1789, they had a huge task before them. The Constitution, the supreme law of the land, granted Congress the authority to create a new government. Although the Constitution gave these men a blueprint that outlined the three separate parts of the federal system—the executive, legislative, and judicial branches—Congress was responsible for creating the actual framework, the positions and departments that would bring the new government to life and conduct the day-to-day functions of governing the nation.

The representatives quickly set about their work. During the spring and summer of 1789, they focused their attention on the executive branch. Congress passed legislation creating the State, Treasury, and War departments to help carry out the responsibilities of the chief executive. Each of these new departments was to be headed by a secretary, appointed by the president and confirmed by the Senate. The department secretaries—who would collectively become known as the cabinet—would meet together to aid and advise the president.

The Judiciary Act

By September 1789, the congressmen were ready to turn their attention to creating the judicial branch. Article III of the Constitution states, "The judicial Power of the United States, shall be vested in one supreme Court, and in such

21

The Preamble and Article I of the U.S. Constitution, ratified by the states in 1788. The document established the fundamental character of the new government; that is, the separation of powers among three branches: legislative, executive, and judicial.

inferior Courts as the Congress may from time to time ordain and establish." With the Judiciary Act of 1789, Congress provided the Supreme Court with one chief justice and five associate justices. It established the inferior—or lower— courts by dividing the nation into 13 districts and 3 circuits, each with its own court.

The federal district courts represented the first rung on the judicial ladder: They were to hold original jurisdiction in (would be the first courts to hear) cases involving the United States or federal officials. That is, in every legal suit in which the United States or an official of the federal government was a party, the case would be brought in a U.S. district court rather than in a state court. The circuit courts, although holding original jurisdiction in a few cases, were primarily appellate courts—that is, they would hear cases on appeal after the district court had ruled.

In addition to establishing these courts, the Judiciary Act provided for the appointment of United States district attorneys (known as U.S. attorneys) and federal marshals. The U.S. attorneys would represent the federal government in the federal district and circuit courts; U.S. marshals would act as the chief federal law-enforcement officers in the districts. Even though these positions were created by the Judiciary Act, U.S. attorneys and marshals were members of the executive branch of the federal government.

The final paragraph of the Judiciary Act provided for the appointment of an official to serve as the chief lawyer for the federal government. It stated: "And there shall be appointed a meet [proper] person, learned in the law, to act as attorney-general for the United States, who shall be sworn or affirmed to a faithful execution of his office; whose duty it shall be to prosecute and conduct all suits in the Supreme Court in which the United States shall be concerned, and to give his advice and opinion upon questions of law when required by the President of the United States, or when requested by the heads of any departments, touching any matters that may concern their departments, and shall receive such compensation for his services as shall by law be provided."

The Judiciary Act explicitly set forth the duties of the attorney general. Like the U.S. attorneys and federal marshals, the attorney general was to be a member of the executive branch. In general, he or she was to represent the United States in all lawsuits brought before the Supreme Court and serve as adviser to the president and executive department heads. In return for these services, the attorney general would receive a salary of $1,500 per year.

The First Attorneys General: Restricted Authority

President George Washington chose his friend and former revolutionary war aide Edmund Randolph to serve as the first attorney general. Randolph was highly qualified to fill the position: He had served as state attorney general for

The Supreme Court building in Washington, D.C. The judicial power of the United States is vested in the Supreme Court and lower federal courts. Congress established the federal court system with the Judiciary Act of 1789, which determined the size of the Supreme Court and the number of federal district courts and courts of appeal.

Virginia and as a member of the Constitutional Convention of 1787, in which he had played a leading role in the discussions concerning the creation of the judiciary. But despite his qualifications, Randolph was reluctant to accept the post. The Virginia lawyer was in debt from the years he had spent as

Washington's aide and believed that he could earn more money for his family by working for private clients.

The president was able to persuade his friend that he could do both jobs. Washington assured Randolph that serving as attorney general would give him additional status: Clients would be eager to hire Randolph as their lawyer if he was also a prominent member of the new government. And because the law only required that the attorney general be present in the nation's capital when the Supreme Court was in session, he could also maintain his private law practice. Randolph accepted Washington's argument. He became the first attorney general and took up his new duties in the capital in February 1790.

Randolph found, however, that his position was a demanding one. Although the Supreme Court did not hear any cases during its first two sessions, the attorney general was kept busy advising the president and the executive department heads. The infant United States was faced with many questions arising over its relations with other nations, and President Washington and Secretary of State Thomas Jefferson frequently turned to Randolph for advice on international law. There was little time to maintain a private law practice to supplement his income.

Attorney General Randolph quickly realized that the provisions of the Judiciary Act of 1789 creating his office were flawed. The act did not provide him with the elements of authority necessary to serve effectively. Fearing that centralized law-enforcement power, focused in the office of the attorney general, might threaten citizens' and states' rights, Congress had consciously restricted the authority, salary, and budget of the attorney general's office. For example, Randolph's annual salary was only a fraction of that given the other executive department secretaries: Secretary of State Jefferson and Secretary of the Treasury Alexander Hamilton received $3,500 and Secretary of War James McHenry received $3,000, whereas Attorney General Randolph was paid only $1,500.

In addition, the attorney general was not granted permanent office space in the nation's capital, nor was he given an operating budget with which to hire a clerk or any staff to assist him. Even though the attorney general was not required to be present in the capital all the time (he was permitted to advise the president and other executive department heads through the mail), the demands of the job made this difficult. The salary disparity, lack of office space and staff, and limited residency requirement were indications that Congress had intended the attorney general to serve only part-time, therefore restricting his ability to exercise unusual power. However, Randolph soon recognized that the federal government needed a full-time attorney.

The final aspect of the Judiciary Act of 1789 that created problems for the new attorney general concerned his relationship with the U.S. attorneys and federal marshals. Although he was technically their superior and responsible for handling any cases appealed to the Supreme Court from their jurisdictions, there were no defined lines of authority or communication between his office and their offices. In short, Attorney General Randolph could not supervise or advise the attorneys and marshals even though they were responsible for initiating and conducting federal cases within the court system.

In December 1791, after serving for two years, Randolph wrote a letter to President Washington detailing some of these problems. He recommended that the attorney general be granted supervision of the U.S. attorneys and that he be given money to hire a clerk. Washington agreed and forwarded the letter to Congress. Unfortunately, Congress failed to act on the recommendation because legislators remained fearful of such a centralization of power.

Randolph continued to serve as attorney general until January 1794, when he resigned to become secretary of state. President Washington replaced him with William Bradford, a successful and well-known lawyer from Pennsylvania. During Bradford's service, the attorney general's responsibilities were relatively few. Bradford served for only a short period, dying in mid-1795 after a brief illness.

Bradford was replaced by Charles Lee, who served in both Washington's and John Adams's administrations. During Lee's tenure, the salary of the attorney general was increased twice; however, it still did not match the amounts granted the other cabinet officers. The first 22 attorneys general continued to supplement their income with a private law practice, even though the duties of the public office steadily increased.

The lack of office space and a staff continued to create problems for the attorneys general and also for the presidents, who needed increasingly closer contact with the lawyer. In 1800, when the capital of the United States was moved to Washington, D.C., the State, War, and Treasury departments were granted office space near the White House. Because Congress did not make any provision for the attorney general, lawyers appointed to that office continued to live and work elsewhere when the Supreme Court was not in session, merely corresponding with the president and cabinet.

When President Madison appointed William Pinckney attorney general in 1811, he requested that Pinckney live in Washington, D.C. Pinckney refused, maintaining his private law practice in Baltimore, Maryland. Three years later, when President Madison found it necessary to insist on the move, Pinckney resigned. Madison appointed Richard Rush of Pennsylvania to fill the office of attorney general, insisting that Rush live in the capital, at least during all periods when Congress was meeting. Rush accepted this requirement, and the next 14 attorneys general followed his example. Although all 14 continued to have private law practices elsewhere, they resided in Washington part-time.

In 1816, in his last annual message to Congress, President Madison related many of the hardships that continued to hinder the attorney general. Madison called upon Congress to provide a suitable salary, office, and clerical staff for the lawyer. He also suggested that the attorney general's office be expanded and that he be given more control over the U.S. attorneys. In short, President Madison recommended that Congress create a new department—a department of law—which the attorney general would oversee. Unfortunately, Congress again refused to act.

William Wirt: An Official Record

When Richard Rush resigned to become minister to England in November 1817, newly elected president James Monroe appointed William Wirt to fill the vacancy. Monroe's choice was an excellent one. Originally from Virginia, Wirt

Lawyer and scholar William Wirt served as attorney general from 1817 to 1829. Wirt compiled the opinions of past attorneys general and combined them with his own in a book that helped to validate the importance of his office in the eyes of Congress.

Aaron Burr recruits followers, ostensibly to colonize western Louisiana. However, in 1807 Burr was accused of treason for plotting to liberate the Louisiana Territory and for planning to become its president. He was later acquitted by a federal court.

had established an extremely successful law practice in Baltimore, Maryland. Prior to his own appointment, Wirt had worked with attorneys general and U.S. attorneys on several particularly important cases. For example, he had been hired by the federal government to help a local U.S. attorney prosecute former senator and vice-president Aaron Burr for treason in 1807, after Burr conspired to set up a new republic in the American Southwest. (Although Burr was acquitted, his treason trial remains one of the most famous in the history of the nation.)

In addition to these credentials, Wirt was a well-known Latin scholar and historian. Prior to his appointment as attorney general, Wirt had written a book called *Sketches of the Life and Character of Patrick Henry*, a biography of the revolutionary leader and orator who had pressed the colonists to revolt in 1775 by declaring "Give me liberty, or give me death!"

Wirt served under Presidents Monroe and John Quincy Adams, finally retiring on March 3, 1829. (He remains the longest-serving attorney general in the history of the office.) From the beginning, his contributions helped to convince Congress that changes in the office's administration were needed. When Attorney General Wirt took office he found no books, documents, or papers of any kind to indicate what his predecessors had done. As a result, he began to compile a brief account of past opinions (the reasons and principles upon which a legal decision is based) and maintained a careful record of his own. He produced a book entitled *Official Opinions of the Attorney General*. The volume was approximately 1,500 pages long; more than 500 of those pages detailed Wirt's own opinions. For example, Attorney General Wirt advised the secretary of the navy about methods of distributing money raised from the sale of seized enemy ships and property during the War of 1812. He also advised President Monroe about the relationship between United States neutrality laws and the revolutionary wars that gave many Latin American nations independence from Spain and Portugal. Other department heads sought Wirt's advice about the sale of public lands to private companies and other matters.

Wirt's volume helped to convince Congress how important—and how busy—the attorney general had become. In 1819 Congress provided the attorney general with a fund for office supplies, fuel to heat the office he rented, and a clerk. Three years later, in 1822, Congress took another step in expanding the prestige of the Office of the Attorney General when it granted him official quarters on the second floor of the old War Department building, near the White House. Succeeding attorneys general maintained that office until 1839, when better quarters were found in the Treasury building.

The frigate United States *(right) fires on the British vessel* Macedonian *in the War of 1812. During the war, Attorney General William Wirt advised the secretary of the navy on distributing money raised from the sale of captured enemy vessels.*

29

Roger Brooke Taney
and the Bank of the United States

During the next four decades many attorneys general served with distinction as the role and responsibilities of the office increased. Attorney General Roger Brooke Taney (1831–33) was a close friend and adviser to President Andrew Jackson; their relationship gave the position of attorney general a new visibility.

Taney provided the president with the 1832 legal opinion upon which Jackson based his refusal to recharter the Bank of the United States. In 1819, the Supreme Court had ruled in the landmark case *McCulloch* v. *Maryland* (argued by Attorney General William Wirt) that the state of Maryland could not tax the Baltimore branch of the national bank out of existence. Maryland lawmakers had used their power of taxation to challenge the right of the federal government to create the bank; the Supreme Court had ruled that the federal government was acting within its constitutional rights, and therefore neither Maryland nor any other state could use state taxation to abolish the federal institution.

However, President Andrew Jackson was himself opposed to the bank. When the time came to reissue the charter upon which the bank was founded, Jackson turned to his attorney general for advice. Taney wrote that the Supreme Court should not be permitted "to control the Congress or the Executive when acting in their legislative capacities, but only have such influence as the force of their reasoning may deserve." In other words, Taney was telling the president that although the Supreme Court had ruled that the original bank charter was constitutional, Jackson was not constitutionally bound to recharter it. President Jackson, a vigorous opponent of the federal bank, acted on Taney's advice and abolished the institution.

Henry Gilpin:
The Opinions of the Attorney General

Henry Gilpin was the next attorney general to leave a distinguished imprint upon the office. Gilpin, a lawyer from Pennsylvania who served under President Martin Van Buren from January 1840 to March 1841, recognized that the record of opinions compiled by William Wirt was extremely valuable. He combined this record with later opinions from the departmental files in a volume entitled *The Opinions of the Attorney General of the United States from*

Attorney General Roger B. Taney (pictured here) issued a legal opinion in 1832 that allowed President Andrew Jackson to abolish the Bank of the United States.

the Beginning of the Government to 1841. Van Buren sent the document to Congress, and the House of Representatives had it printed under its authority. For the next 50 years, subsequent volumes were printed and distributed by private publishers. Since 1890 the Government Printing Office has published the opinions, making them an important part of the United States's official record.

Caleb Cushing: Expanded Responsibilities

In 1853, following a period of relative inactivity in legal affairs, President Franklin Pierce appointed the ambitious and versatile Caleb Cushing attorney general. Like William Wirt, Cushing came to the office with a well-established reputation. He was the son of a wealthy Massachusetts family. The author Nathaniel Hawthorne, the poet John Greenleaf Whittier, and the influential newspaper editor and abolitionist William Lloyd Garrison had been among his boyhood friends. Rather than pursue a literary or publishing career as they had, Cushing chose to attend Harvard Law School for a year and then to serve an apprenticeship with a Massachusetts attorney. He was admitted to the Massachusetts bar in 1821. After practicing law for 13 years, he was elected to Congress, where he served 4 terms. In 1843, President John Tyler appointed Cushing United States commissioner to China. Three years later, after the United States declared war on Mexico, Cushing led a regiment that he had raised and equipped himself. Before the war was over, he had become a brigadier general.

Immediately following Cushing's appointment, Congress raised the attorney general's salary to match that of the other members of the cabinet. He was now expected to devote his full time to the duties of the office. Cushing took up residence in Washington, D.C.; since then, attorneys general have lived either in Washington or in the nearby Virginia and Maryland suburbs.

Cushing was both energetic and ambitious. Despite an already heavy work load, he attempted to bring more of the government's legal work under his supervision. He sent two reports to the president, recommending an expansion of the judiciary system and an increase in the power of the Office of the Attorney General. For the judicial system, Cushing called for the establishment of intermediate courts of appeal, and for his own office, the right to take responsibility for all cases before the lower courts. Despite President Pierce's support, Congress refused to act on these recommendations.

32

The talented and ambitious Caleb Cushing served as attorney general from 1853 to 1857. Legislators resisted Cushing's numerous attempts to gain more responsibility for his office.

The War Years

Jeremiah Sullivan Black served as attorney general from 1857 until December 1860, just prior to the outbreak of the Civil War. When several Southern states, opposed to federal dominance and angered by Northern politicians' efforts to restrict slavery, threatened to leave the Union, Black offered an opinion that set the stage for the coming national tragedy. He reminded President James Buchanan that the power of the federal government is spelled out in the Constitution. In fulfilling the functions defined in that document, the federal government of the United States is sovereign, or supreme. All remaining powers, however, are left to the states. In performing these remaining functions, the states are sovereign. Neither the federal government nor the states can go beyond their constitutional limits.

According to Black, should any state declare itself independent of the United States, the president could do relatively little. Because the Constitution does not mention this matter, the president does not have the constitutional right to recognize that independence; nor does the Constitution give the president the right to release the state from its federal responsibilities.

Attorney General Jeremiah Sullivan Black (1857–60, seated at far right) in-formed President James Buchanan (fourth from left) that the president was powerless to prevent the Southern states from seceding from the Union. This opinion set the stage for the Civil War.

In addition, Black warned that any attempt to declare war on a state would be unconstitutional; such an action would be similar to expelling a state from the Union. Although the federal government has the constitutional right to defend itself against aggression on federal property, it may not attempt to punish the citizens of a state for political misbehavior. Black's opinion was highly unpopular with many who wanted President Buchanan to act vigorously in the face of the Southern states' threat to secede from the Union.

President Abraham Lincoln chose Edward Bates (March 1861 to July 1864) and then James Speed (December 1864 to July 1866) to serve as attorney general during the difficult years of the Civil War. Both men served honorably, providing the president with legal advice during the crisis. In 1861, during Bates's tenure, Congress finally accepted the need for a more efficient court system. That year, it granted the attorney general the right to supervise the

U.S. attorneys and marshals. The law now required them to report to the attorney general. It also permitted the attorney general to advise the U.S. attorneys and to employ additional counsels—private lawyers with particular expertise—to assist the U.S. attorneys in fulfilling their duties.

A Legal Department for the Nation

Congress once again expanded the responsibilities of the office in 1868 when it ordered the attorney general to represent the United States in all cases brought before the Court of Claims. This court had been added to the judicial system in 1855 and held jurisdiction in any case in which claim was brought against the federal government for unpaid salary, property seized for public use, unmet contractual obligation, or personal injury. Originally, the legislation that created the Court of Claims also provided for a solicitor who would handle all cases before the court. When the 1868 legislation transferred this responsibility to the attorney general, the Office of the Solicitor of the Court of Claims was abolished. The Office of the Attorney General was given two new assistant attorneys general, to be appointed by the president, and an increased clerical staff.

By 1870 it had become clear that efficiency and economy demanded the creation of a unified federal legal department. Over the course of the preceding 40 years, many of the executive departments had requested and received their own legal staff. For example, in 1830, Congress created the Office of the Solicitor of the Treasury, granting the solicitor the right to work with the U.S. attorneys to bring suit against individuals or negligent officials who owed the federal government money. In 1836, Congress created the Office of Auditor of the Treasury for the Post Office Department. This official was responsible for directing all suits to enforce payment of money due the post office. In 1863, Congress provided for a solicitor for the War Department, and in 1865, a solicitor and naval judge advocate for the navy. A year later, Congress created the Office of Examiner of Claims within the State Department. Despite their different titles, these officials were basically serving as lawyers for their departments.

On April 27, 1870, Congressman Thomas A. Jenckes of Rhode Island introduced a bill into Congress that would consolidate the legal business of the United States under one department, headed by the attorney general. Jenckes provided a compelling argument. He noted that the creation of so many independent legal offices was creating chaos and confusion. In one instance, the

In 1870, Congressman Thomas A. Jenckes of Rhode Island was able to convince his fellow legislators to integrate the legal business of the country into one department by creating the Department of Justice.

paymaster of the army was given an opinion by one legal officer, while one of his aides was given a completely different opinion on the same subject by another legal officer. Jenckes noted that "neither obtain[ed] the opinion of the Attorney General, who ought to have been consulted. The consequence is a difference of opinion and a difference of advice in each case upon the same statute."

Jenckes was also quick to point out that this inefficiency and duplication of effort was quite costly. Although the federal government employed a great number of lawyers, it was not always getting the best representation. Jenckes concluded:

> We have now this great anomaly: the Attorney General is bound to conduct all the cases of the United States in the Supreme Court of the United States; yet in the majority of instances he never hears of the cases until the printed record is in his hands, and there is no place in Washington to which he can go to ascertain the history of the case. Under the law as it stands the Solicitor of the Treasury

may advise the district attorneys in certain cases. The Attorney General has a general supervision over the district attorneys in all cases; but this general supervision and control has never been defined by law or usage in any opinion of the Attorney General. Hence the district attorneys have a divided responsibility. . . . [The Attorney General] is responsible as the chief law officer of the Government. If any error is committed we shall know who is chargeable with it.

The time was finally right. As the government's legal business had expanded, fears about centralized federal authority had diminished. The crisis surrounding the Civil War had given Americans a new appreciation for the federal government. They realized that too much state authority had nearly destroyed the Union. Although American citizens were not ready to accept the idea that the federal government should have greatly expanded power, they were less fearful that centralized power was necessarily a threat to liberty. They recognized that a balanced and efficient combination of local, state, and federal government could work together. When the members of Congress were confronted with the logic of Jenckes's argument, they were ready and willing to put their former fears aside and establish a centralized law department. And so, in June 1870, Congress created one department to handle all the government's legal business. That department is the Department of Justice.

A cartoon from the Progressive Era (1893–1917) shows President Theodore Roosevelt—who was popularly known as the "trust-buster"—on Wall Street in New York City, battling the giants Jay Gould, James J. Hill, J. P. Morgan, John D. Rockefeller, Sr., and the Oxnard brothers, who were among the era's most influential financiers and industrialists.

THREE

Growing with
the Nation

On July 4, 1870, the people of the United States had good reason to celebrate the nation's birthday with new optimism. The bloody Civil War that had threatened to permanently divide the country and end the dream of a united people under one federal government had been over for five years. Political disputes over how the Union would be restored had been largely resolved. The people of the United States entered a new decade with a renewed spirit of energy and unity that would usher the nation into the next century.

Amos Tappan Akerman had reason that day to be particularly optimistic about the nation. Although born in New Hampshire, Akerman had been raised in Georgia. He had grown to love the South and had voluntarily served in the Confederate army during the Civil War. When the South lost the war, many people feared that the region would be punished unmercifully and that Southerners would be denied responsible positions in the government. But President Ulysses Grant's appointment of Akerman as the nation's 31st attorney general on June 23, 1870, proved these fears unfounded.

Akerman was chosen to serve as the head of the new Department of Justice, which was formally established on July 1. The new department would have a large staff and would assume many new responsibilities. Clearly the nation was ready for change, and the appointment of a Southerner to this important

cabinet post signaled the hope that this transformation could occur without further sectional strife.

After 1870, the United States expanded as thousands of people left the farms of rural America to develop the vast resources of the West and to live and work in the new urban centers that were springing up in the East and Midwest. Once in the cities, these men and women joined with thousands of European immigrants who came to this country to share in the promise of prosperity. Entrepreneurs such as industrialists Andrew Carnegie and John D. Rockefeller, meat-packing magnate Gustavus Swift, and financiers E. H. Harriman, James J. Hill, and J. P. Morgan employed these skilled and unskilled laborers to create new industries, transportation systems, and technologies and methods of production. They changed American society from the rural, agrarian country of the 19th century into an urban, industrial 20th-century giant.

These changes had an enormous effect on the life of all Americans. New laws and attitudes about the role of the federal government emerged as people attempted to apply 18th-century democratic political ideals to this modern society. Few executive departments reflect these changes more clearly and fully than the Department of Justice. Over time, as citizens' concerns were expressed in the passage of new laws, the Department of Justice developed a number of specialized divisions to enforce these laws. The history of the Civil, Criminal, Land and Natural Resources, Antitrust, Tax, and Civil Rights divisions and the Immigration and Naturalization Service parallels and reflects the development and growth of the United States well into the 20th century.

The Act to Establish the Department of Justice placed the attorney general at the head of a department that had no clearly defined structure. It mandated

U.S. railroad construction reached a high point when the Union Pacific, building westward from Nebraska, and the Central Pacific, building eastward from California, met at Promontory Point, Utah, on May 10, 1869. The Justice Department developed a number of specialized divisions to enforce the laws passed by Congress in response to the changes in society brought on by new transportation systems and industries.

that the attorney general would have the assistance of a solicitor general, "who, in case of a vacancy in the office of Attorney-General, or in his absence or disability, shall have power to exercise all the duties of that office," and the help of two assistants. However, the legislation did not include any divisions of responsibility or specialization.

At first, a Justice Department lawyer's assignment to a case was made without regard for specialization. If a suit required particular expertise in an area, the department hired an expert to assist the lawyer. However, it soon became clear that some division of responsibility and departmental specialization was necessary.

The Civil Division

The first example of departmental specialization involved civil law and cases arising from claims against the federal government. In 1868, even before the department was created, Congress had recognized that cases involving claims against the government—particularly those concerning property that had been damaged or confiscated during the Civil War—made up a large portion of the business of the attorney general. Congress had provided for the temporary appointment of an assistant to concentrate on settling these claims. When the Justice Department was created two years later, the law did not specifically mention this assistant. However, it was clear that one of the attorney general's two assistants would continue to concentrate on these cases.

Property claims resulting from the Civil War dominated the department's business in its early years. Southerners sued the government because their property had been seized in the first years after the war. Many Northerners also had property claims because of wartime damage, and private companies had claims arising from their wartime contracts to provide weapons and supplies.

Other claims resulted from the daily activities of the government. As the nation experienced tremendous growth during the last decades of the 19th century, the federal government was increasingly involved in commercial activities. These included buying the supplies necessary for running the government; selling land and other commodities; constructing buildings; shipping; and lending money. Whenever a grievance arose concerning such an activity and a lawsuit was brought before the Court of Claims or the lower courts, the Department of Justice was responsible for representing the government's interests.

Amended **PETITION.**

To the Honorable Commissioners of Claims,

Under the Act of Congress of March 3, 1871, Washington, D. C.:

The *Amended* Petition of [1] *Margaret A Dement*

respectfully represents:

That she [a] citizen of the United States, and resides at present at or near
[2] *Jenkins Ferry Grant Co. Ark.*
and that she resided when this claim accrued at or near [3] *Jenkins Ferry*

That she has a claim against the United States for property [4] *taken*

for the use of the army of the United States during the late rebellion at (or near)
Jenkins Ferry, in the county of *Grant*, and State of
Arkansas

That the said claim, stated by items, and excluding any and all items of damage, destruction, and loss, (and not use,) of property; of unauthorized or unnecessary depredations by troops and other persons upon property, or of rent or compensation for the use or occupation of buildings, grounds, or other real estate, is as follows:

No. of Item	QUANTITIES AND ARTICLES.	VALUE.
1	6 Head cattle weighing 400 lbs each 1st Jan 14 $	
	viz 2400 lbs a/c 5¢ per lb	$120
2	400 lbs Bacon 20¢ per lb	80
3	200 Bushels corn @ $1 per Bushel	200
4	3000 Rails at $1.00 per 100	30
5	3000 feet pine oak & lumber at $2.00 per M	60
6	Carpenter tools	25
7	9 Yearlings (calves) at $8 per head	72
8	2 Calves at $5 Each	10
9	30 Bushels Wheat $2 per Bush	60
	Total,	$657

Note: 1. Give full names of all the petitioners.
2. Give the residence of each petitioner.
3. Give the former residence of each petitioner.
4. "Taken," or "furnished."

A Southerner's petition claiming that the listed items were confiscated for use by Union troops during the Civil War. After the Civil War, many Southerners brought suit against the U.S. government for confiscated or destroyed property. In its early years the Justice Department concentrated on resolving such claims.

Frequently, such cases demanded a lawyer with specialized legal knowledge. As the department grew and more attorneys were added to the staff to try these cases, a specific division within the department was established. From shortly after the turn of the century through 1933, the office was called the Admiralty and Civil Division. For a brief period in the 1930s, the division was referred to as the Claims Division, but this title did not seem satisfactory. Finally the title *Civil Division* emerged and has remained the official title for the office.

The Civil Division today employs nearly 500 attorneys. It is headed by an assistant attorney general and divides its responsibilities between a number of branches and offices. Although the division continues to handle claims brought against the federal government, many of the circumstances that generate these lawsuits have changed. The factual basis for civil suits against the federal government reflects changes in American citizens' attitudes about the responsibilities of their government. In one case in the mid-1980s, for example, the plaintiffs asserted that the Parole Commission (the Justice Department board that grants parole—conditional release—and supervises parolees) and the Bureau of Prisons (the Justice Department bureau responsible for overseeing all prisoners within the federal penal system) should be held liable for a murder committed by a former prisoner who went on a killing spree after being paroled. Civil Division attorneys successfully defended the interests of the federal government against this claim of liability.

Civil Division personnel have also acted on behalf of the federal government in cases involving defense contractor fraud. In 1987 they won a $2.5 million settlement in a case against Stencel Aero Engineering Corporation for overcharging and falsifying invoices in connection with the manufacture and installation of ejector seats in U.S. Navy jets. In the late 1980s Civil Division attorneys also opposed the attempt by several major corporations to declare bankruptcy in order to avoid paying damages to workers who became ill after being exposed to asbestos. Department arguments in the asbestos cases aimed to prevent the companies from shifting the financial responsibility for medical care for the workers onto the American taxpayer.

The Criminal Division

Commercial claims and litigation (contesting in court) were not the only concern of the Justice Department during its formative years. As the department expanded in Washington and the attorney general began to

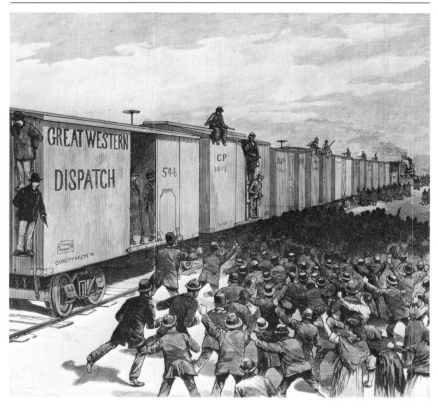

In 1886, striking railroad workers attempt to prevent a train, guarded by the Justice Department's U.S. marshals, from starting. The emergence of labor unions and workers' demonstrations in the late 19th century aroused fears of crime and violence in America.

exercise direct supervision over the U.S. attorneys and other federal law-enforcement authorities, it became clear that the laws defining federal criminal offenses (as opposed to state criminal offenses) were haphazardly enforced and difficult to prosecute.

The history of the development of these laws provides a partial explanation for the problem. In addition, the two-tiered system of American criminal justice that permits prosecution of certain crimes by state authorities and others by the federal government provides another explanation.

The early settlers brought with them to America much of the cultural heritage that they had known in England. Part of that heritage was the English system of common law that set forth ordinary criminal offenses. Since colonial times, each state has enacted its own statutes defining criminal activity within its boundaries. As a result, prosecution of common criminal offenses such as murder, robbery, and fraud has been largely the responsibility of state authorities. (Today, each state typically has prosecutors with titles such as district attorney, state's attorney, or commonwealth attorney, who are responsible for representing in the state courts the interests of the state in prosecuting criminal offenses committed against citizens of the state and their property.)

The U.S. Constitution actually defines only one crime—treason. Article III, Section 3, describes treason as the following:

> Treason against the United States, shall consist only in levying War against them, or in adhering to their Enemies, giving them Aid and Comfort. No Person shall be convicted of Treason unless on the Testimony of two Witnesses to the same overt Act, or on Confession in open Court.
>
> The Congress shall have Power to declare the Punishment of Treason . . .

The Constitution also implies that the federal government is responsible for prosecuting those people accused of counterfeiting and of piracy on the high seas. However, under its mandate to pass laws that are necessary to carry out its proper functions, Congress has passed legislation that defines other federal crimes. For example, Congress enacted its first criminal statute in April 1790. This law established the punishment for treason and made the commission of murder in any area under the jurisdiction of the federal government—such as a military fort, arsenal, or dockyard—a federal offense. Death by hanging was the prescribed punishment for both treason and murder committed on federal property. (Even today, crimes committed on land that belongs to the federal government are prosecuted by U.S. attorneys rather than by state prosecutors.) Over time, Congress continued to pass laws that granted federal prosecutors, rather than state or local authorities, jurisdiction in prosecuting certain crimes, particularly those that were committed in more than one state. However, these laws were not immediately collected into one body of law; they remained separate pieces of legislation.

In 1883, Attorney General Benjamin Brewster, a Pennsylvania attorney appointed by President Chester Arthur, recommended that the criminal statutes be consolidated into one criminal code. Attorney General Brewster's reform suggestion reflected a common concern. People were worried about the increase in crime and violence in America. Worker unrest associated with the emerging American labor union movement had produced a number of bloody riots and confrontations between strikers and police as laborers agitated for increased salaries, shorter workdays, and improved working conditions. Fear was spreading that many of the new immigrants streaming into the country to work in American factories brought with them dangerous ideas about socialism (the political and economic philosophy that advocates collective ownership and administration of the means of production and distribution of goods) and anarchism (a political philosophy that seeks the abolition of all government).

These concepts appeared to threaten American political and economic institutions. The assassination of President James A. Garfield in 1881 by a

Mourners view the coffin of President James A. Garfield in the Rotunda of the Capitol in 1881. The president's assassination heightened people's fears that criminals threatened the political stability of the nation.

disappointed office seeker added to fears that criminals threatened the political stability of the United States. The worst fears of many people were confirmed five years later during an incident known as the Haymarket Riot. On May 4, 1886, there was an organized workers' demonstration in Chicago's Haymarket Square. When police tried to disperse the crowd of 1,500, a bomb exploded in the police ranks. Eleven people were killed in the ensuing riot, and four men were later hanged for the death of the policemen.

Because Congress was slow to act on the reform suggestion, Attorney General Brewster assumed personal responsibility for supervising a small staff that concentrated on criminal cases. Finally, in 1909, Congress gathered all the criminal statutes into one criminal code. This criminal code was added to the general U.S. Code adopted in 1928, the same year that Attorney General John Sargent created the Criminal Division within the Department of Justice. As with the other major divisions, the Criminal Division was headed by an assistant attorney general.

The Criminal Division immediately assumed responsibility for litigating all cases involving a violation of the federal criminal laws. Today, some of the other divisions of the department—such as the Civil Rights, Tax, Antitrust, and Land and Natural Resources divisions—have responsibility for litigating criminal violations of the laws that they enforce. However, the primary responsibility for prosecuting federal criminal offenses remains with the Criminal Division.

The federal criminal cases for which the Department of Justice is responsible include cases of treason; violations of American neutrality, such as organizing a military force to be used against a friendly nation; counterfeiting; threats against public officials; theft of government property; bribery of a government official; extortion; harboring an escaped prisoner; obstruction of the mails; mailing of obscene material; transporting stolen goods across state lines; and use of the mails or wire communications facilities (such as the telephone) in aid of a scheme to defraud.

In recent years, to prosecute cases involving organized crime, Justice Department attorneys have made use of statutes that prohibit a conspiracy to commit a federal offense, racketeer-influenced and corrupt organizations (RICOs), and continuing criminal enterprises (CCEs). Additional federal laws prohibit the possession or distribution of a wide variety of narcotic and dangerous drugs. Once convicted of a violation of the laws against organized criminal activity or narcotics trafficking, a criminal, in a separate civil forfeiture proceeding, may lose the property and assets acquired through the illegal activity.

President Herbert Hoover (right) and Attorney General John Sargent in 1928. Faced with mounting criminal activity in the United States, Sargent created the Criminal Division within the Department of Justice.

In January 1988, a U.S. Secret Service agent displays some of the evidence in what was at the time the largest seizure of counterfeit money ever—$16 million, confiscated in Houston, Texas. The Justice Department's Criminal Division is responsible for prosecuting counterfeiters.

The Organized Crime Drug Enforcement Task Force (OCDETF) program supplements the work of both the U.S. attorneys and the Criminal Division. It consists of 13 regional task forces that employ the personnel and expertise of 11 federal agencies, in cooperation with state and local investigators and prosecutors, to target and eliminate major narcotics trafficking and money-laundering organizations (organizations that hide cash, generated by illegal activity, in seemingly legitimate businesses). Participants in OCDETF include the Drug Enforcement Administration; Federal Bureau of Investigation; U.S. Customs Service; Internal Revenue Service; Bureau of Alcohol, Tobacco and Firearms; U.S. Coast Guard; U.S. Marshals Service; and the Immigration and Naturalization Service.

Approximately 400 attorneys are employed by the Criminal Division at Justice Department headquarters in Washington, D.C. They are divided into sections that assume responsibility for specific types of prosecutions and activities in support of the U.S. attorneys around the country. Criminal Division attorneys are actively involved in the prosecution of international terrorists, pornographers, corrupt public officials (at both the state and federal levels), organized-crime figures, major narcotics traffickers, and those who threaten the international security of the United States by illegally exporting munitions or militarily significant technology. Criminal Division attorneys prosecute fraud and investigate Nazi war criminals who entered the United States without disclosing their past. Attorneys in the Office of International Affairs of the Criminal Division negotiate international agreements on criminal law enforcement and coordinate international extradition cases (cases in which an alleged criminal is surrendered by one country to another with jurisdiction to try the charge).

The matters that occupy attorneys of the Criminal Division often involve both civil and criminal laws. For example, at the same time that Civil Division attorneys are pursuing efforts to curb overcharging and waste by government contractors, attorneys from the Fraud Section of the Criminal Division are involved in a coordinated effort known as Operation Ill Wind to prosecute defense contractors who illegally obtained information to help them get government contracts. Similarly, several sections in the Criminal Division actively investigate and prosecute criminal activity by members of groups involved in organized crime, while at the same time forfeiture proceedings may be initiated by the Criminal Division's Assets Forfeiture Office against the illegal proceeds of that activity.

Cases against racketeers and money launderers often involve violations of the tax laws as well as the criminal statutes. In 1986, Justice Department

Stock trader Ivan Boesky arrives at federal court in New York City in 1987. Boesky, believed to be one of the the richest men in the world, pleaded guilty to charges stemming from insider trading, an activity that is in violation of the securities laws.

attorneys prosecuted members of five "families" of organized crime that operated in many cities. On March 21, 1986, Michael Franzese—a self-confessed "captain" in the Colombo organized-crime family—pleaded guilty to federal racketeering and tax conspiracy charges. Under the plea agreement, Franzese was sentenced to spend 10 years in prison, pay a fine of $35,000, and provide $10 million in restitution to the victims of his crimes. An additional $4.7 million of Franzese's property was seized and forfeited to the federal government. Justice Department lawyer Edward McDonald, who built the case against Franzese, stated that it was unusual for an alleged Mafia member to plead guilty. McDonald remarked, "I think they realized that the government had put together a very strong case."

Justice Department lawyers also vigorously prosecute financial crimes. In 1985, the Department of Justice obtained a plea of guilty from E. F. Hutton & Co., Inc., to charges of mail and wire fraud in a scheme that defrauded banks of interest on the firm's accounts. E. F. Hutton paid a fine of more than $2 million. In the late 1980s, the United States attorney's office in Manhattan initiated a series of significant cases against Wall Street investment advisers who violated securities laws by trading stocks based upon information known to insiders but not to the general investing public. Attorneys from the Criminal Division's Fraud Section and assistant U.S. attorneys actively prosecuted those who were accused of defrauding failed banks and savings and loans institutions in Texas, Oklahoma, and other areas of the country.

In recent years the Justice Department has increasingly prosecuted criminal activity that crosses international boundaries. Criminal Division attorneys in the Office of International Affairs have forged a vital link with prosecutors and law-enforcement officials around the world to ensure cooperation in the fight against international terrorism, drug trafficking, and financial crimes. In the 1980s, the department was involved in the investigation and prosecution of many espionage cases. In 1985, for example, the department prosecuted former navy communications specialist John Walker and his network of spies. Walker ultimately pleaded guilty to espionage charges and cooperated with federal prosecutors by testifying against Jerry Whitworth, another navy man charged with selling secrets to the Soviet Union. John Walker was willing to plead guilty and to cooperate in the Whitworth case in exchange for the promise that his son, Michael Walker, would not receive a life sentence for his participation in the crime.

The United States attorney's office for the District of Columbia has a special responsibility for such cases and was also involved in the highly publicized prosecution of Jonathan Jay Pollard, a former navy counterintelligence analyst who was convicted of espionage in June 1986. Pollard had provided classified

(continued on page 57)

Navy enlisted man Michael Walker (in rear seat) leaves the federal courthouse in Baltimore in November 1986 after being sentenced to 25 years in prison. The Justice Department prosecuted Walker and his father, former U.S. Navy communications specialist John Walker, for selling secrets to the Soviets.

The United States v. Ramon Melendez

The United States Attorney's Office for the District of Columbia plays a unique role in law enforcement. Because of the federal government's special interest in the safety of government officials and foreign visitors to the nation's capital, and because the Constitution gives Congress the authority to govern the District of Columbia, the U.S. attorney for Washington, D.C., prosecutes not only all federal crimes committed in the district but also those crimes that in other jurisdictions would be prosecuted by local authorities. In addition, the U.S. Attorney's Office in Washington has the authority to indict international terrorists and others who commit federal offenses outside the country's borders, even if the perpetrators have no ties to any state in the United States.

One Friday morning in March 1984, Assistant United States Attorney Pamela B. Stuart was acting as the intake assistant for the section of the U.S. Attorney's Office in Washington, D.C., that handles federal crimes. It was her responsibility to review incoming cases presented by law-enforcement agents for prosecution and to review drafts of affidavits (sworn statements in writing) to be presented to the court in support of requests for search warrants (legal permission to search private property for stolen goods or illegal possessions).

That morning, Stuart was visited by several distinguished-looking military officers in full uniform. Her visitors had a simple request: Could she arrange for a warrant (a magistrate's written permission) to be issued for the arrest of one Ramon Melendez, who was then being detained in a jail in Spain but was due to be released the following Tuesday? Quickly, the officers, who represented the Office of Special Investigations of the U.S. Air Force, the Naval Intelligence Service, and the Army's Criminal Investigation Division, laid out their case.

Melendez, a native of the Philippines, had worked for the U.S. Army during the Vietnam War. He had learned to use forged papers identifying him as a U.S. military officer to purchase goods and to cash checks at U.S. military installations around the world. Over the years, the officers estimated, Melendez had personally stolen more than $6 million from the U.S. government.

Melendez was now believed to be working with a criminal organization based in Manila that had a member employed by the San Francisco post office. Through this connection, the organization had stolen millions of dollars worth of U.S. Treasury checks intended to pay the salaries of military personnel stationed in Asia. The crime ring provided Melendez with forged papers identifying him as the officer to whom each check was made out, and Melendez cashed the checks.

A sharp-eyed sales clerk at the Air Force post exchange (the "PX") at Torrejon Air Force Base, near Madrid, had recognized Melendez

Pamela B. Stuart, former assistant U.S. attorney, in front of the U.S. Courthouse in Washington, D.C., in 1989.

from a wanted poster. Melendez was arrested at last and was now being held by the Spanish authorities.

Stuart asked the officers if Melendez had ever been in Washington, D.C., or even in the United States. No, they replied, and they reminded her of the infrequently invoked statute that allows for prosecution in the District of Columbia of persons who commit offenses against the United States but have never actually set foot in this country. With the question of jurisdiction resolved, the U.S. Attorney's Office quickly went to work.

Stuart helped prepare the papers to obtain the necessary arrest warrant and contacted an attorney in the Office of International Affairs in the Justice Department's Criminal Division. With his help, she learned that it would be necessary to translate the documents into Spanish. She would also have to prepare a request for the provisional arrest of Melendez under the extradition treaty between Spain and the United States, which could be presented to the Spanish court before Melendez was due to be released on Tuesday. Under the terms of the treaty, Melendez would then be detained by the Spanish authorities for an additional 45 days. During that time, Stuart would have to present evidence to a U.S. grand jury that would enable it to return an indictment charging Melendez with all of the crimes he had committed against the United States; to obtain documents and affidavits from witnesses that would establish probable cause to believe that Melendez had committed the crimes; to prepare an affidavit setting forth the prosecutor's overview of the evidence and the applicable U.S. law to satisfy the Spanish court that Melendez's actions would be a crime in Spain; and to arrange for all of these documents to be translated into Spanish and certified by the attorney general, the secretary of state, and the Spanish embassy in Washington.

Lawyers and investigators from each of the armed services and agents from the U.S. Secret Service who were responsible for investigating the forgery of signatures on U.S. Treasury checks located witnesses in Japan, the Philippines, Germany, and Spain. These people were flown to Washington to testify before the grand jury. Experts in the forgery of military identification papers went to work on the accumulated evidence and prepared reports identifying Melendez as the man pictured on the forged papers. They also identified his fingerprints on some of the documents. Authorities in Germany searched the room Melendez had occupied prior to his trip to Spain and found a typewriter that experts linked to some of the documents Melendez had with him at the time of his arrest. Within a few weeks, evidence supporting a 154-count indictment had been assembled and presented to the grand jury. The grand jury voted to return the indictment charging Melendez with a variety of federal crimes including forgery, theft from the mails, and impersonation of a military officer.

Because of the need to have affidavits from witnesses to support each of the 154 counts of the indictment, the evidence supporting the official request for the extradition of Melendez comprised a stack of documents one foot tall. Two translators working night and day finished translating the material into Spanish the day before the documents were due in Madrid. After officials at the Justice Department and the State Department affixed seals to the documents identifying them as official U.S. government papers, the consul at the Spanish embassy affixed a seal certifying that the documents had been officially presented in Washington by the U.S. government. Stuart carried her precious cargo on an overnight flight to Madrid and presented the documents to the Spanish Foreign Ministry the next day.

The Spanish court eventually approved the extradition of Melendez, and United States marshals returned him to Washington in November. His case was assigned to Judge Oliver Gasch of the United States District Court. On the advice of his court-appointed lawyer, Melendez accepted a plea bargain—an agreement whereby the defendant pleads guilty to a lesser charge. Melendez was sentenced to a term of 15 years in prison. Because he had been wanted by the U.S. government for 20 years, and because he was one of few who had then been prosecuted in connection with the thefts from the San Francisco post office, Melendez was profiled on the CBS news program "Sixty Minutes."

Stuart left the U.S. Attorney's Office in 1985 to become a senior trial attorney in the Justice Department's Office of International Affairs, where she handled widely publicized international extradition cases for two years. She is now in the private practice of law in Washington, D.C.

The Italian cruise ship Achille Lauro *leaves Port Said, Egypt, in October 1985 after the capture of the four Palestinian gunmen who had hijacked the ship and murdered an American passenger. Criminal Division attorneys participated in the prosecution of the hijackers.*

(continued from page 53)
documents to Israel over a period of two and a half years. Criminal Division attorneys were involved in the attempt to bring to justice those who hijacked the *Achille Lauro* cruise ship and murdered an American citizen, Leon Klinghoffer, in 1985. And in March 1989, an Arab named Fawaz Yunis was convicted in Washington, D.C., for the hijacking of a Royal Jordanian airliner in Beirut, Lebanon, under a new law that allows for the prosecution in the District of Columbia of terrorists who direct their activities against the United States or American citizens anywhere in the world.

The Land and Natural Resources Division

As the nation expanded during the last decade of the 19th century and the first decades of the 20th century, federal lawsuits did not necessarily fit into the two neat categories of civil and criminal divisions. The resultant need for new areas of legal specialization led the Justice Department to create additional divisions to allow department attorneys to concentrate in these areas.

During the late 19th century, many Americans began to call for the government to take a more active role in protecting public lands and natural resources. In the earliest years of the Republic, when these resources had seemed limitless, private citizens and businesses had been relatively free to develop and utilize them. Neither the federal government nor private citizens gave much thought to conserving resources for the future needs of the nation. By the last decades of the 19th century, however, the finite nature of these resources was becoming clear. The 1890 census reported for the first time that the United States no longer had an unbroken line of frontier—a boundary beyond which land was virtually unexplored and undeveloped.

Lawmakers first became aware of the impending danger to forests on federally owned land in the West. Huge tracts of timberland were being destroyed as mass migration westward created a great demand for lumber for new construction and for creation of a vast railroad system to transport goods and people. Because there were no laws protecting the trees on public lands, private individuals and lumber companies were free to enter the forests and cut the timber. Government officials became particularly concerned about red cedar and live oak trees because shipbuilders used this wood to build U.S. Navy vessels. In 1813, in order to protect this valuable resource, Congress passed a law authorizing the president and the secretary of the navy to protect timberlands. The law prohibited any cutting of red cedar or live oak on public land. In 1831, the law was expanded to include all kinds of trees on public lands.

The Department of the Interior, a federal agency created in 1849 to oversee various land-related government affairs, was given responsibility for the administration and protection of threatened lands and resources. However, the attorney general, acting through the U.S. attorneys, was responsible for prosecuting any individuals who broke protective laws. Because he had very limited control of the U.S. attorneys, the attorney general could do little to enforce these laws before 1870. But after the Department of Justice was created, this responsibility was given new priority. In 1886, reflecting the new national concern for resources, the Justice Department brought suit against the Sierra Lumber Company of California for cutting down 16,000 trees on public land. The case continued through appeal until 1892, when the Sierra company was fined $15,000. Although the settlement was much smaller than the actual value of the lumber, the private company had been soundly punished and prevented from any further plundering of the natural resource. And other companies had been given notice that the Justice Department would prosecute those guilty of violating resource-protection laws.

Other resources were gradually given legal protection as well. Just as the trees were needed for naval ship construction, oil reserves located on public

Lumberjacks cut down a tree in the early 20th century. As the American frontier extended westward, settlers cut down forests to clear land and to provide lumber for construction. The Land and Natural Resources Division of the Justice Department was created to prosecute people who were accused of cutting trees on public land and violating resource-protection laws.

lands had to be preserved for use by the military. And as people recognized that scenic areas such as the Grand Canyon and Yellowstone National Park should be preserved for future generations, the government set aside millions of acres of such lands to form the National Park System, making these areas off limits to private development so that all Americans could enjoy them. Any individual or company attempting to exploit these resources for private gain was liable to prosecution under federal law—which meant that lawyers for the Justice Department tried the case.

In addition to protecting public lands and resources, the Justice Department was responsible for verifying the title (legal ownership) of all property purchased by the federal government. When the government purchases a piece of land—for oil, land, or timber reserves, or for the building of a post office, military post, or national park—the title must be researched to ensure that the proper owner is paid. This process can require a great deal of work. Researchers must trace the sale of the land back several generations to make certain that the land title is *free and clear* (a legal term that means that there are no financial claims against the land).

Finally, Justice Department lawyers found themselves increasingly busy with cases resulting from the government's troubled relationship with American Indians. Many times, for example, tribes charged that the federal government had purchased land from them based on an unfair valuation. Decades after a sale, an Indian tribe could claim that when the purchase of tribal lands was made the tribe did not receive a fair price. These cases often took years to settle and required lawyers with solid knowledge of property, treaty, and contract—and sometimes tribal—law.

In 1910, recognizing that the department needed a division of lawyers who specialized in this type of litigation, Attorney General George W. Wickersham created the Land Claims Division. By 1965, the scope of the office had expanded to cover so many areas that its name was changed to the Land and Natural Resources Division.

Today, this division is one of the most active branches of the Justice Department. Its responsibilities have evolved to reflect all types of environmental concerns. The 260 lawyers assigned to the Land and Natural Resources Division handle litigation concerning issues such as public land development, Indian claims, and wildlife resource protection. To prosecute polluters, the division works closely with the Environmental Protection Agency, an executive department created in 1970 to set standards for clean air and water and to regulate the handling and disposal of poisons and other hazardous wastes. The division also has primary responsibility for litigation under the "Superfund"

Barrels of hazardous waste are scattered around a New Jersey dump. The Land and Natural Resources Division works with the Environmental Protection Agency to prosecute violators of toxic-waste disposal regulations and clean air and water standards.

program that Congress created in 1980 to spur the cleanup of toxic waste dumps. In a 1988 case handled by Land and Natural Resources Division attorneys, a federal judge in Kentucky fined Ashland Oil Company $2.25 million—one of the largest environmental fines ever levied—for a 700,000-gallon diesel fuel spill on January 2, 1988, into the Monongahela River that affected drinking water in several states.

The Antitrust Division

At the same time that people were becoming concerned about preserving America's natural resources and public lands, they also began to worry about preservation of the nation's basic economic structure. Although people such as Carnegie, Rockefeller, Hill, Swift, Harriman, and Morgan were largely viewed as geniuses—true heroes who were fulfilling "the American dream"—they were also viewed with some alarm. The giant industries they created threatened to monopolize (assume exclusive control over) the economy and put an end to fair competition between businesses. The public increasingly called upon the federal government to protect citizens from unfair business practices and to ensure that a few industrial, commercial, banking, and transportation giants did not gain a stranglehold on the nation's economy.

Congress reacted to these concerns by passing a number of laws prohibiting monopoly. The Sherman Antitrust Act of 1890, the Federal Trade Commission and Clayton acts of 1914, and a variety of other laws established the rules of fair trade and competition. Taken together, these laws granted the federal government the right to prosecute those who attempt to create a monopoly or to act "in restraint of trade" through such unfair methods of competition as price fixing (setting artificially low prices in order to drive competitors from the market), illegal boycotts (the refusal to deal with a certain person, store, or organization), and illegal mergers (the absorption of one corporation by one or more others, or the combination of two or more corporations). Naturally, any criminal prosecution under these statutes fell to the Department of Justice. (Today, the Department of Justice and the Federal Trade Commission—an agency formed in 1914 to make sure that competition remains free and fair—share responsibilities for civil actions brought to enforce the antitrust laws.)

These issues were vitally important during the Progressive Era (1893–1917), and the court cases that emerged were viewed as battles waged between good and evil, right and wrong, industrial "giants" versus "the little guy." At issue was America's most fundamental concept of how government and society should be organized: Should talented individuals be permitted to create huge companies that might triumph over their smaller competitors, free from all government restraint and regulation? Or should the federal government serve as the watchdog of the economy and regulate these companies?

It took many years of litigation to answer antitrust questions and to determine the proper balance between the private and public sectors. The Justice Department spent many decades bringing cases under the antitrust

Andrew Carnegie emigrated from his native Scotland in 1848 and made his fortune in the iron and steel industries. At the end of the 19th century, many American industrialists were suspected of conspiring to stifle business competition, prompting Congress to pass the Sherman Antitrust Act of 1890. The Justice Department was called on to prosecute people who attempted to monopolize the American economy.

laws against the railroad, sugar, beef, steel, and banking industries. Slowly, the opinions issued by the courts that heard these cases began to define the rules.

At first, attorneys general tended to handle antitrust cases personally. As the number of cases increased, however, a special assistant was assigned to help prepare the cases and follow them through the appellate process until they reached the Supreme Court. Ultimately, as new corporate structures emerged, making the cases amazingly complex, the department recognized a need for another specialized division. In 1933, the Antitrust Division was formally created with a large staff of lawyers who specialize in corporate law.

Although the Antitrust Division has grown a great deal since its creation, it continues to perform much the same function. The 266 lawyers assigned to the division litigate cases that involve the protection of free trade and competition. They protect American citizens from practices that would increase the cost of products and services as a result of potential or actual loss of competition in the industry.

On January 7, 1987, for example, the department charged four antique dealers with violating the Sherman Antitrust Act. These dealers had agreed among themselves to rig bids at public auctions in Pennsylvania, New Jersey, Delaware, and Maryland. They agreed not to bid against each other—thus keeping down the price paid to the original owner. Once one of the four dealers purchased the goods, the group would have its own auction; they would then divide the proceeds among themselves. This practice is a violation of laws that forbid price fixing and bid rigging.

Antitrust lawyers have also handled cases involving mergers in the airline, railroad, and film-production industries. Antitrust Division lawyers study the impact of proposed mergers to determine their possible effects on consumers. For example, when the MacAndrews and Forbes Group, Inc., wanted to buy Metrocolor Laboratories from Lorimar Telepicture in 1986, Justice Department attorneys said no. MacAndrews and Forbes already owned one primary film laboratory (a facility that produces the 35-millimeter and 70-millimeter prints for major motion pictures). If they had been permitted to buy Metrocolor, they would then control two of the three laboratories that do this work. As a result of Justice Department action, the proposed merger did not occur.

Justice Department attorneys do not always disallow mergers, however. In 1985–86, Justice Department attorneys worked with the Department of Transportation (DOT) when Texas Air Corporation proposed the purchase of Eastern Airlines. Department attorneys advised DOT to approve the merger, because Pan American Airlines offered a shuttle service along the East Coast that would continue to compete with the Texas Air/Eastern Airlines service.

The Tax Division

The attorney general's office has a long history of involvement in tax cases, beginning in 1790, when federal marshals and U.S. attorneys were involved in the Whisky Rebellion, the refusal of western Pennsylvania farmers to pay a federal excise tax on the whiskey they produced. The uproar over this issue lasted four years and finally involved the use of the state militia, a visit to the area by Secretary of the Treasury Alexander Hamilton, and prosecution of some participants for treason. This pattern was to be repeated again and again; many agencies became associated with tax cases, and the lines of authority were frequently unclear.

Long before the Sixteenth Amendment to the Constitution, added in 1913, authorized the collection of federal income taxes, the U.S. government relied upon taxes as a source of revenue. In 1820, Congress granted the secretary of the Treasury responsibility for recovering any debts owed the federal government. This law divided departmental jurisdiction: The Treasury Department brought suit against a tax evader, but lawyers from the Justice Department tried the case. President Andrew Jackson was the first to recommend that the entire process be handled by one department. However, Congress did not act on that suggestion, and the Treasury Department and the attorney general continued to share responsibility for prosecution.

Following the creation of the Justice Department, tax cases began to involve extremely complex constitutional questions. During the Progressive Era, many reformers called for an income tax on individuals and corporations to supply revenue for the government. Between 1870 and 1933, the Supreme Court heard dozens of cases dealing with the tax question. These cases helped determine the tax status of charitable foundations and of American citizens who live and own property abroad; the right of the government to tax municipal bonds issued by cities and states; and the extent of congressional power to tax businesses through tariffs (taxes on imported and, sometimes, exported goods).

By 1933, it had become clear that these cases had more to do with constitutional issues than with actual revenue collection. On June 10, 1933, responding to the changed circumstances, President Franklin D. Roosevelt issued an executive order establishing the Tax Division of the Department of Justice. Congress recognized the necessity of such a division and did not offer any objection.

Today, the Tax Division continues to oversee all suits arising from violation of the internal revenue or tax laws. The division never formulates tax policy,

President Franklin D. Roosevelt created the Justice Department's Tax Division by executive order in 1933.

nor does it establish tax rates. These functions remain the responsibility of the Treasury Department and its Internal Revenue Service (IRS). The 328 Tax Division attorneys become involved only when a suit is brought, either by or against the federal government, over a tax question. Such cases frequently involve thousands of dollars owed to the federal government in taxes. Increasingly, Tax Division attorneys work closely with their colleagues who prosecute criminal cases against organized-crime figures, drug smugglers, and money launderers. For instance, in a 1986 case, *United States* v. *Carlos Ernesto Armenta LaFaurie,* a Colombian drug dealer was forced to turn over to the U.S. government vast amounts of money he had deposited in a Swiss bank account and to pay nearly $4 million in taxes on these profits. The efforts of the Tax Division not only supplement the efforts of the criminal prosecutors but, in cases involving otherwise legitimate businesses, help to make the tax burden on all Americans more equitable.

66

The Immigration and Naturalization Service

" 'Give me your tired, your poor,/ Your huddled masses yearning to breathe free.' " These words, from "The New Colossus," a poem by Emma Lazarus, adorn the base of the Statue of Liberty and welcome all immigrants who enter the United States by way of New York harbor.

Although the Statue of Liberty and the words carved in its base were not dedicated until 1886, they symbolize the ideal that had motivated citizens of other nations to journey to the shores of the United States since the earliest days of the nation. For more than 100 years, the United States had welcomed thousands of immigrants, recognizing that the talents and labor of these people would help to make the nation strong. Although immigrants frequently faced hardship and discrimination in their newly adopted country, they recognized the potential for success and advancement.

During these years, the federal government exercised very little control over immigration. Although there were a few instances where exclusionary laws were passed to limit immigration and to protect American labor during the 19th century, the issue of immigration was largely left to state and local control. Finally, President Benjamin Harrison signed an act on March 3, 1891, that established federal control over this important area. This legislation created the position of superintendent of immigration, under the direction of the Treasury Department, and charged this officer with overseeing the inspection of immigrants. All new arrivals were to be temporarily detained at Castle Garden, New York (in later years at Ellis Island, in New York harbor), where they underwent medical examinations and background checks. From 1891 on, immigrants who suffered from contagious diseases, had criminal records, or were paupers (and thus unlikely to find employment because of their lack of skills) were denied entry into the United States. The new law also authorized the superintendent to deport any immigrant who entered the United States without going through this procedure.

In 1895, to help the superintendent of immigration fulfill his responsibilities, Congress created a Bureau of Immigration and changed the title of the superintendent to commissioner general of immigration. This change, although somewhat helpful, did not completely solve the problems associated with the new immigration controls. Many legislators recognized that these issues were not directly concerned with the duties associated with the Treasury Department. Therefore, in 1903, Congress transferred all responsibility for immigration affairs to the newly created Department of Commerce and Labor. Three years later, additional legislation specified that the administration of the immi-

Immigrants arrive at Ellis Island, New York, in 1902. Today, the Justice Department's Immigration and Naturalization Service helps qualified aliens enter the country and assists immigrants with the process of becoming citizens when they decide to remain in the United States.

gration service would remain with Commerce and Labor, whereas the field force for investigating and prosecuting illegal immigrants would fall to the Justice Department.

Throughout the next 30 years, various attempts were made to reform this system and make it more efficient. During some periods, the Justice Department had no responsibility for matters involving immigration. When the Department of Commerce and Labor split into two separate departments in 1913, the Labor Department took full responsibility for immigration issues. In that same year, the Labor Department developed a separate division to deal with naturalization, the process by which immigrants become American citizens.

The immigration and the naturalization services operated separately, within the Department of Labor, until 1933, when they were merged under Executive Order 6166. The new Immigration and Naturalization Service was headed by a commissioner. This arrangement continued until April 1939, when President Franklin D. Roosevelt proposed that the entire service be transferred from

Labor to Justice. The transfer was accomplished on June 14, 1940, and from that time on responsibility for both immigration and naturalization has fallen to the Justice Department.

Today, the division operates under the title of the Immigration and Naturalization Service (INS). The INS is responsible for helping qualified aliens enter the country and for denying admission to those who are unqualified because of health problems, criminal records, or lack of employable skills. Once new arrivals are granted admission to the United States, the INS continues to supervise them, ensuring that they receive any help and information they may need. The INS also provides assistance with the naturalization and citizenship process to any immigrants who wish to remain in the United States permanently. Finally, the INS is responsible for apprehending and deporting any aliens who enter the United States illegally or whose authorization to stay has expired.

The Immigration and Naturalization Service is an extraordinarily large and busy division within the Justice Department. The INS has offices in more than 30 major U.S. cities and in many foreign countries. The Immigration Reform and Control Act of 1986 gave the INS new responsibilities involving amnesty (pardon for immigrants who entered the country illegally), employer sanctions (punishment of employers who hire—and frequently exploit—illegal aliens), and the rights of temporary workers. As the federal government attempts to deal with the increasing pressure of thousands of immigrants fleeing poverty and political repression throughout the world, the INS will assume an increasingly important role in maintaining the balance between national interests and the ideals of justice.

The Civil Rights Division

The newest division of the Justice Department, the Civil Rights Division, is also one of the most active and most important. For many Americans, particularly blacks, the division's creation, in 1957, represented a new commitment by the federal government to protect and guarantee their rights as citizens. As the division has expanded, other groups—women, Hispanics, the elderly, Native Americans, the physically disabled, and members of other minority groups—have come to rely on the Civil Rights Division to protect their rights as well.

The civil rights of all American citizens are specifically guaranteed by the Bill of Rights (the first 10 amendments to the Constitution), the Thirteenth,

Robed and hooded Ku Klux Klan members hold a meeting in 1915. The Klan, a white supremacist group, was just one of many southern groups that violated the rights of black Americans in the years after the Civil War. The Justice Department has been prosecuting individuals accused of racial discrimination since 1870.

Fourteenth, and Fifteenth amendments (which, respectively, abolished slavery; prohibited the denial of citizenship without due process of law; and made it illegal to deny a citizen the right to vote on the basis of race, color, or previous condition of servitude), and a variety of federal laws aimed at protecting civil rights and civil liberties. These amendments and laws guarantee that all Americans can live, work, and participate in the electoral process without barriers imposed on the basis of their race, religion, sex, age, or national origin.

Although the Civil Rights Division was the last of the major divisions to be created, its roots reach back to the earliest days of the Justice Department. In

1870, federal officials were justifiably concerned about the treatment of former slaves in the South. Shortly after the creation of the Justice Department, Attorney General Amos Tappan Akerman was given a $50,000 Senate appropriation with which to fund departmental investigations of racial discrimination.

For the next seven years, until Reconstruction (the post–Civil War period during which federal authorities exercised considerable control in the South) was formally ended in 1877, the Justice Department played an active role in investigating and prosecuting individuals and groups—particularly the Ku Klux Klan—who violated the rights of black Americans. In 1877, however, when the last federal troops and officials were withdrawn from the South, this activist role began to diminish. Between 1877 and 1897, the Supreme Court heard a few civil rights cases, but it was increasingly clear that the southern states were going to be relatively free to create their own methods for dealing with race relations.

In 1897 this hands-off attitude was confirmed when the Supreme Court ruled that segregation—the separation of the races—was constitutional. In the case of *Plessy* v. *Ferguson*, the court said that the principle of "separate but equal" facilities for the races was acceptable under the Constitution. Specifically, the court ruled that railroads could legally provide separate accommodations for

A blacks-only movie theater in Leland, Mississippi, in 1939. Segregated facilities prevailed throughout the South until the Supreme Court ruled in 1954 in Brown v. Board of Education of Topeka *that segregation was unconstitutional.*

71

white and black passengers: As long as the accommodations were "equal" in quality, according to the court, the separation was not racial discrimination.

Although *Plessy* v. *Ferguson* dealt only with public transportation, the "separate but equal" doctrine was applied to all areas of life. Unfortunately, the Justice Department and the federal government largely ignored the inequities that developed as a result. Clearly, American society—and southern states in particular—chose not to provide equal facilities for both races. School systems, housing, transportation, and public accommodations for black citizens were separate but definitely not equal to those provided for whites.

The Criminal Division assumed responsibility for prosecuting civil rights cases. (It did this because many of these cases—such as lynchings—were prosecuted under criminal statutes.) However, most such matters received little attention or priority: When the cases involved crimes committed by whites against blacks, white juries tended to declare the accused not guilty—thus making the proceedings a waste of the department's time.

This situation continued until 1954, when the Supreme Court ruled in *Brown* v. *Board of Education of Topeka* that segregation in public schools was

President Dwight D. Eisenhower signs the Civil Rights Act of 1957. This legislation enabled the Justice Department to safeguard the rights of black citizens through its Civil Rights Division.

inherently unequal. In this reversal of *Plessy* v. *Ferguson*, the Court ruled that separation of the races based on skin color was unconstitutional. The Court's ruling in *Brown* created a sense of panic and rebellion in many states. The Justice Department was faced with a landslide of cases, many challenging the government's right to enforce the decision and force the desegregation of American society.

Three years later Congress passed the Civil Rights Act of 1957, aimed at reinforcing the Court's ruling in *Brown* and providing the federal government with new methods to protect the rights of black Americans. The Civil Rights Act empowered the Justice Department to prosecute anyone attempting to deprive a black citizen of his or her voting rights. The act also established the Civil Rights Division within the Justice Department and created the bipartisan Civil Rights Commission to investigate civil rights violations and recommend legislation to further protect these rights.

On December 9, 1957, Attorney General William P. Rogers formally created the Civil Rights Division. The new division immediately took over the records, files, and backlog of 143 civil rights cases from the Criminal Division. From this point on, lawyers and investigators within the new division pursued an active role in searching out and prosecuting any violations of the civil rights legislation.

Over the next three decades, the activity of the Civil Rights Division came to represent the federal government's commitment to equal rights. The mandate of the division grew to include the protection of many more minority groups. Today, the division employs nearly 200 lawyers, all actively involved in protecting and preserving the individual liberties of American citizens.

When Amos Tappan Akerman accepted the position of 31st attorney general of the United States—responsible for overseeing the creation of the Department of Justice—he had little reason to suspect that someday the department would include seven major divisions and would employ thousands of people. However, he and his contemporaries did recognize the vital importance of a unified department of law, ready and able to defend the interests of the American government and the rights and interests of the American people.

This understanding has guided the development of the department from its earliest days. Throughout the last decades of the 19th and into the 20th century, whenever governmental activity or responsibility has increased, so too has the size and scope of the Department of Justice. As the watchdog of both national interests and individual rights, the growth of the Justice Department reflects the continuing concern of American society to maintain the democratic ideal.

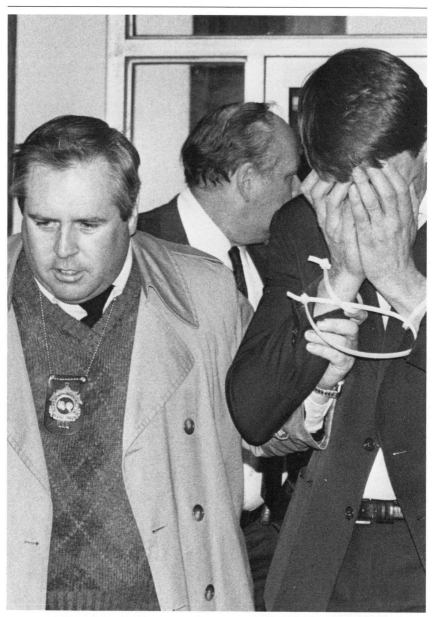

An agent of the Justice Department's Drug Enforcement Administration clutches a suspect in a $1.5 billion cocaine smuggling ring at New York's Kennedy Airport in 1987. The DEA is charged with enforcing the nation's drug laws.

FOUR

The Long Arm
of the Law

The United States does not have a national police force. Yet if most Americans were asked, they would undoubtedly describe the Federal Bureau of Investigation (FBI) and the Drug Enforcement Administration (DEA) as just that. Americans have come to count on the special agents of the FBI when children are kidnapped, when airplanes are hijacked, when illegal drugs enter our communities, and whenever criminal activities occur that are beyond the scope and capabilities of local law-enforcement agencies. The agents of the DEA have specialized responsibility for enforcing the laws against drug trafficking and abuse. An integral part of the Department of Justice team, these agencies owe their authority to acts of Congress, presidential instructions, and directives from the attorney general.

The FBI and the DEA together represent the investigative arm of the Department of Justice. In many respects, they are the most controversial divisions within the department. Many people have worried about the power held by these two divisions—especially about the potential for the abuse of power that the FBI represents. Americans are justifiably concerned that such a secret organization, with the power to investigate and keep files on citizens, may threaten civil liberties. However, the service performed by these agents is clearly a necessary and important one. It remains the ultimate responsibility of the attorney general and other Justice Department officials to make sure that the power granted these special agencies is neither abused nor subverted.

The Federal Bureau of Investigation

The Judiciary Act of 1789 granted the U.S. attorneys the authority to investigate violations of federal law and to collect evidence for presentation in the courts. This system, in effect, made every U.S. attorney not only a prosecutor but also a detective—and quickly proved unworkable. Many federal attorneys were not equipped, by training or experience, to perform these duties. The problem was made more difficult when several attorneys general ruled that money allocated for the operation of U.S. district and circuit courts could not be used to fund investigative work or to hire professional detectives.

As director of the FBI from 1924 to 1974, J. Edgar Hoover made the FBI the nation's top crime-detection agency. However, his abuses of power—particularly the harassment of left-wing activists and suspected Communists—made his legacy controversial.

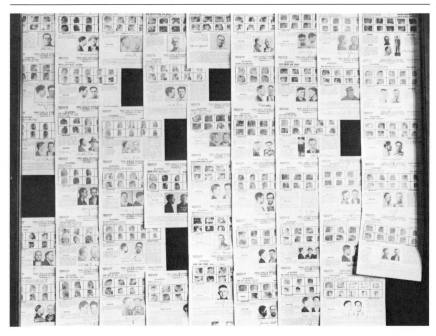

A bulletin board in Ames, Iowa, shows FBI wanted posters in 1936. The bureau displays such posters in post offices to alert the public to fugitive felons.

In 1870, when the Department of Justice was created, Congress recognized this problem. One year later, Congress appropriated $50,000 for use by the attorney general to detect and prosecute crimes against the federal government. At first, Attorney General Amos Tappan Akerman relied on members of the Secret Service—a Treasury Department bureau created in 1865 to combat counterfeiting—to aid in this process. In 1875, however, Attorney General George Williams appointed four detectives to his department, and federal attorneys were given permission to hire "special agents" when they were needed.

By 1907 this system not only proved beneficial but also showed signs that it could be put to even greater use. In that year, Attorney General Charles Bonaparte tried to convince Congress that a special investigative agency, responsible for collecting and classifying information about criminal activity and sharing this information with state authorities, would be of great value. Congress appointed a special committee to look into the matter, but it was clear that legislators were not very enthusiastic about the idea of a powerful national police force. Some feared the potential power of this kind of agency:

In 1933, gangster George "Machine Gun" Kelly (second from left) surrendered to FBI agents in Memphis, Tennessee, crying, "Don't shoot, G-men! Don't shoot!"—thus coining a nickname for Hoover's agents.

Who would control it? If it was part of the executive branch, could the president order agents of the force to investigate congressmen who opposed the president on certain issues? Other congressmen argued that the federal government would be paying for an agency that was of primary aid to state governments; they charged that this would be an unfair and unnecessary use of limited federal funds.

Despite these fears, on July 26, 1908, Attorney General Bonaparte created the Special Agents Force, a small and relatively inactive group. In March 1909, Bonaparte's successor, George W. Wickersham, issued his own order, changing the name to the Bureau of Investigation. This bureau, too, remained relatively small, and it received very little public attention. In 1924, however, Attorney General Harlan Fiske Stone reorganized the bureau and appointed a young lawyer, J. Edgar Hoover, as its director. Within a few years the public became aware of bureau activity and was very pleased with the results, as

G-men (the popular name for the bureau's agents, meaning government men) were involved in a number of exciting cases, such as the capture of the infamous gangster George "Machine Gun" Kelly in 1933; the fatal shoot-out with John Dillinger, the most notorious criminal the FBI has ever hunted down, in 1934; and the 1935 shoot-out in Florida with Ma Barker, who had led her four sons on a spree of kidnappings, robberies, and murders.

Working closely with U.S. attorneys and local officials, Hoover's agents caught bank robbers, mobsters, and kidnappers, despite the technicality that the agents did not have any law-enforcement authority. In 1934, after public concern about the agency had largely disappeared, bureau agents were given authority to carry weapons, serve subpoenas (orders to appear in court) and warrants (court orders authorizing detainment, seizure, or search), and make arrests. The following year the bureau's name was changed to the Federal Bureau of Investigation.

During World War II and the cold war (a period of hostile diplomatic relations between the United States and the Soviet Union in the following decades),

The FBI named outlaw John Dillinger public enemy number one in 1933. The following year, Dillinger was finally shot by FBI agents in Chicago after a girlfriend betrayed his whereabouts.

In 1988, FBI agents lead suspected drug traffickers to the federal courthouse in New York City. More than 200 people were arrested in a cooperative effort by U.S. and Italian law-enforcement officials and charged with taking part in a major heroin importing ring.

fears of Communist infiltration ran rampant in the United States. FBI agents were credited with the capture of alleged saboteurs and spies such as Ethel and Julius Rosenberg. FBI surveillance of suspected Communists and subversives continued into the 1960s, as civil rights protests, campus demonstrations against the Vietnam War, and calls for women's liberation became increasingly vehement and frequently violent. Hoover construed such political protest to be un-American, and the FBI investigated and kept records on many of the leaders of these movements—often using illegal methods, such as wiretaps, to collect evidence that could be used against them. After Hoover's death in 1972, lawmakers became aware of the abuses of power that had occurred during his tenure, and subsequent directors instituted reforms to renew public trust in the FBI's activities.

Today, as the principal criminal investigative arm of the federal government, the bureau concentrates primarily on investigating organized crime (including drug trafficking), foreign counterintelligence, white-collar crime, and terrorism. The FBI works closely with other Justice Department divisions, other federal agencies, and many state and local law-enforcement groups and offers its services in police training, crime laboratory work, and fingerprint identification to other law-enforcement agencies.

The Drug Enforcement Administration

The history of federal drug-enforcement activity dates back to the beginning of the 20th century. The 1914 Harrison Narcotics Act established a tax on imported opium and coca products and required everyone who shipped, handled, sold, or prescribed the drugs to be registered with the government. The Treasury Department's Internal Revenue Service was given official responsibility for the enforcement of the law, because it was a tax law. This duty fell to 162 agents in the IRS's Miscellaneous Division. In 1920, these agents, numbering 1,550, were reorganized into the Prohibition Unit, which had been formed to enforce the Eighteenth Amendment, or Prohibition—a ban on the manufacture, transport, and sale of alcohol.

In 1927, the Treasury Department created the Bureau of Prohibition, a separate division from the IRS, to take over the Prohibition Unit's drug and alcohol law-enforcement duties. Three years later the Treasury Department created the Bureau of Narcotics to concentrate on the drug trade.

In the 1960s many people experimented with recreational drugs, and the use of illegal substances such as marijuana, LSD, and heroin began to cause concern. In 1966, the Bureau of Drug Abuse Control of the Department of Health, Education and Welfare's (HEW's) Food and Drug Administration (FDA) joined forces with the Treasury's Bureau of Narcotics to combat the growing use of drugs in America. For two years, Treasury and FDA agents worked together. Then, in 1968, authority for these activities was transferred to the Justice Department, and the Bureau of Narcotics and Dangerous Drugs was created. In 1973, President Richard Nixon created the Drug Enforcement Administration by combining the Bureau of Narcotics and Dangerous Drugs with four other federal drug law-enforcement agencies. Then in 1982, Attorney General William French Smith gave the FBI shared jurisdiction over drug

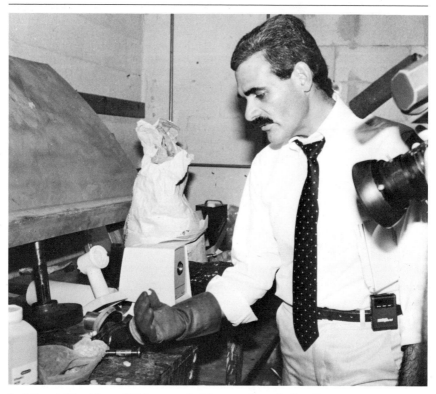

In Miami, Florida, a DEA agent holds up a Quaalude after agents raided a lab in 1988 and seized more than nine million tablets. The DEA works with local law-enforcement agencies to combat the production and smuggling of illegal drugs.

offenses and ordered the DEA's administrator to report to the director of the FBI within the Justice Department.

Today, the DEA's 2,300 special agents serve not only in the United States but also in foreign countries where drugs are produced and exported. The DEA stations many agents in Latin American countries and in other locations around the world near the bases of operation used by international traffickers. In some countries in Latin America, DEA agents have assisted local law-enforcement efforts to wipe out crops of illegal drugs and the factories where these drugs are processed. These agents are the front lines of American troops fighting the war on drugs.

The DEA has its headquarters in Washington, D.C., and maintains field offices around the country. Scientists at the agency's seven forensic science laboratories perform drug analyses, study fingerprints and photographs, and examine clothing and other objects for drug residues. In addition, the DEA's approximately 300 compliance investigators enforce the regulations concerning the manufacture and distribution of prescription drugs.

The DEA works with other federal agencies to combat narcotics smuggling and distribution networks in the United States and in foreign countries. These include the U.S. Customs Service, the U.S. Coast Guard, and the IRS. In addition, the DEA often works alongside state and local police forces to combat the growing drug problem in America.

Robert F. Kennedy, brother of President John F. Kennedy, served as attorney general from 1961 to 1964. Chief among his concerns was the protection of civil rights.

FIVE

The Largest Law Firm in the Nation

The Department of Justice employs thousands of lawyers, economists, investigators, agents, and law-enforcement and prison officials. It is the nation's single largest law firm, and yet it serves only one client: the federal government. Protection of this client requires a complex bureaucratic organization that is capable of administering and enforcing the law, providing legal counsel to the federal government, and protecting American citizens from those charged and convicted of committing crimes.

All Justice Department employees are either in the competitive or the excepted federal civil service. Those who are part of the competitive service hold nonlegal positions and are required to take a standardized competitive examination before they may be considered for employment. The excepted service, on the other hand, is made up of lawyers and law students who are hired based on their educational background and experience. Approximately one-half of these lawyers work in Washington, D.C.; the others are located throughout the country.

The Attorney General

The Office of the Attorney General remains at the pinnacle of the Justice Department. Although the attorney general now serves as the head of this huge administrative complex, the actual job description has changed very little

Richard Thornburgh, former governor of Pennsylvania, was appointed attorney general in 1988. In a 1989 case, Thornburgh defended the government's position requiring federal employees to undergo random drug testing.

since the position was created in 1789. The attorney general remains the chief legal officer of the United States, representing the nation in legal matters, giving advice to the president and, when requested, to the executive department heads, and appearing before the Supreme Court when cases are of particular importance or significance. In early 1989, for example, Attorney General Richard Thornburgh personally defended the position of the U.S. government in a case in which federal employees challenged a program requiring them to undergo random drug testing.

The attorney general is aided in fulfilling his or her responsibilities and in the overall administration of the Justice Department by three individuals: the deputy attorney general, the associate attorney general, and the solicitor general.

The Deputy Attorney General

The deputy attorney general is technically second in command. Appointed by the president, he or she is authorized to assume the top position when the attorney general is absent. Usually, the deputy attorney general is an expert in criminal law. In the past, officers with such expertise have traditionally been given direct authority over those bureaus, divisions, and offices that deal primarily with criminal matters—for example, the Criminal Division, the United States Marshals Service, the Bureau of Prisons, and the Immigration and Naturalization Service. In addition to these responsibilities, the deputy attorney general has supervisory responsibility for the United States Parole Commission and administrative control of the department's own attorney-hiring programs.

The Associate Attorney General

The associate attorney general, on the other hand, is typically a lawyer whose expertise rests in the area of civil law. As a result, he or she has authority over the Antitrust, Civil, Civil Rights, Land and Natural Resources, and Tax divisions. He also supervises the United States Trustees' Office (the office that oversees the administration of all bankruptcy cases) and the Foreign Claims Settlement Commission (the office that deals with any claims brought by U.S. nationals for loss of property in a foreign country). The associate attorney general is considered next in command after the deputy attorney general. In the unlikely event that both the attorney general and deputy attorney general are absent, the associate attorney general assumes responsibility for the department.

The Solicitor General

The solicitor general is the third major aide to the attorney general and, in many ways, is one of the most visible members of the Justice Department. The solicitor general and his or her assistants appear before the Supreme Court, representing the United States in all cases except those in which the attorney general chooses to appear. The solicitor general is responsible for deciding which cases the Justice Department will ask the Supreme Court to review; which cases, lost before lower courts, should be appealed; and what position the department should take on cases being heard by the Supreme Court.

The Office of Legal Policy

The Office of Legal Policy serves as the attorney general's policy development group. This think tank studies issues, advises the attorney general on matters relating to departmental policy, and works to produce legal reform. The Office of Legal Policy also identifies qualified candidates for federal judgeships.

The Office of Professional Responsibility

The Office of Professional Responsibility serves as an internal departmental watchdog. Members of this office investigate any allegation of misconduct—either ethical or criminal—brought against a member of the department. They also provide opinions to lawyers formerly employed by the department concerning the propriety of representing clients who have business with or cases before the Justice Department.

The Justice Management Division

Headed by the assistant attorney general for administration, the Justice Management Division is responsible for matters pertaining to organization, management, and administration of the Justice Department. Any senior management official within the department can turn to this division for assistance with budgeting and financial management, personnel training and control, data processing and telecommunications, procurement of equipment, and security problems.

Office of Liaison Services

The Office of Liaison Services serves as the central point of contact between the Justice Department and many other governmental and private groups. The principal groups that call upon the Office of Liaison Services for information include the following: state governors, legislators, and attorneys general; local officials such as mayors, chiefs of police, and prosecutors; foreign courts and law-enforcement agencies; and, finally, private groups such as the American Bar Association (a professional organization composed of lawyers admitted to any state bar), the International Association of Chiefs of Police, and numerous law schools and universities that train lawyers.

Community Relations Service

The Community Relations Service's mediators and conciliators help to resolve disputes concerning the violation of antidiscrimination statutes or any alleged

Contemporary Justice and Woman, *a 1937 mural, is located in the lobby of the Department of Justice Building. The mural's center panel depicts the figure of Justice cutting the chains of tradition that bound women; in the background, a freed woman walks into the light of a new world. Flanking scenes illustrate women engaged in newfound roles, such as sculptor, dancer, student, and scientist. The bottom panel represents the traditional roles of women, such as mother, housekeeper, cook, and laborer in the fields.*

discrimination based on race, color, or national origin. The service also works with communities to avoid such problems.

The Office of Legal Counsel

The attorney general is often presented with presidential and cabinet requests for straightforward advice about the law; at other times, he or she is presented with situations in which two or more executive departments are in disagreement. The Office of Legal Counsel, headed by an assistant attorney general, is responsible for drafting these legal opinions. In addition, this office may draft its own opinions or give advice in response to queries by government agencies, offices within the Justice Department, and presidential staff and advisers. The office also provides legal advice to the executive branch on all constitutional questions.

The Office of Legislative Affairs

Although the attorney general is not officially responsible for providing Congress with legal advice, the department does have contact with the legislative body. The assistant attorney general in charge of the Office of Legislative Affairs serves as a liaison between Congress and the Justice Department. This office is in charge of preparing reports and recommendations about legislation pending before Congress. Some of these reports acquaint congressmen with the Justice Department's view of the legislation; for example, a report might be issued stating that, in the opinion of the attorney general, a new law under consideration is unconstitutional. (Although only the Supreme Court can ultimately rule on the constitutionality of a law, Congress relies on the attorney general for advice that will help avoid challenges to the laws it passes.) On other occasions, the office may write reports to inform members of the Justice Department about new laws and congressional activity. Finally, the Office of Legislative Affairs provides assistance and support for all departmental and judicial nominees during the confirmation process.

The Office of Intelligence Policy and Review

The Office of Intelligence Policy and Review advises the attorney general on national-security activities and provides government agencies such as the FBI,

Central Intelligence Agency (CIA), and the Departments of Defense and State with advice concerning national-security law and policy.

The U.S. Marshals Service

The United States Marshals Service has grown tremendously since the first 13 marshals were appointed by President George Washington in 1789. U.S. marshals provide protection for federal judges, attorneys, and jurors during all proceedings in federal courts. They ensure the safety of witnesses through the Witness Protection Program: When a witness must change his or her identity and relocate his or her family as a result of cooperation with federal prosecutors, U.S. marshals assist in all aspects of the witness's transition to a

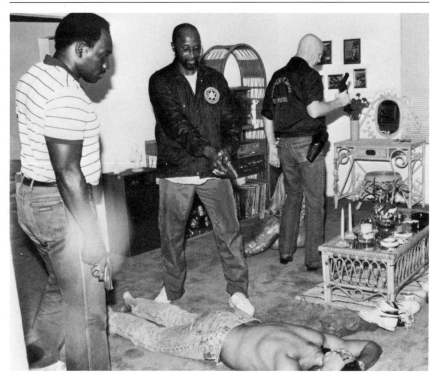

Deputy U.S. marshals arrest William Martinez, a fugitive wanted by the DEA for drug trafficking, at an apartment in Miami, Florida, in 1989. The U.S. Marshals Service captures or aids in the capture of approximately 14,500 criminal fugitives each year.

Deputy Attorney General Nicholas de B. Katzenbach (right) attempts to negotiate with Alabama governor George Wallace, who, flanked by state highway patrolmen, blocks the entrance to the University of Alabama in 1963. The appearance of federal marshals later convinced Wallace to step aside and allow black students to enroll in the school.

new life. U.S. marshals also execute court orders and arrest warrants. They transport criminals between courts and prison and capture federal fugitives.

When criminals are convicted, many times their property—if gained illegally—is seized and then sold by the federal government. In these cases, marshals are responsible for the seizure, storage, and sale of the property, which ranges from airplanes used to smuggle drugs into the country to homes, cars, jewelry, and other personal property paid for with illegally gained money.

Finally, the U.S. marshals play a role in maintaining and restoring order. The marshals work with local and state authorities when riots or mob violence threaten to disrupt communities. This role was particularly evident during the 1960s, at the height of the civil rights movement. In 1962, for example, when

Mississippi governor Ross Barnett defied a court order and refused to allow James Meredith—a black student—to enroll at the University of Mississippi, Attorney General Robert F. Kennedy sent federal marshals to enforce the order. When the marshals were outnumbered by a violent white mob, federal troops were sent in.

A year later, Governor George Wallace of Alabama stood in the doorway of a university building and blocked the enrollment of black students at the University of Alabama. In this case, the governor stepped aside when federal marshals appeared to escort the youths into the building.

The Executive Office for U.S. Attorneys

The 94 U.S. attorneys are responsible for the prosecution of criminal offenses against the United States, the representation of the U.S. government in civil

In January 1989, U.S. Attorney Rudolf Giuliani of New York (second from left) and Attorney General Richard Thornburgh (third from left) announced the formation of a government task force to investigate securities and commodities fraud.

actions in which the government is a party or has an interest in a particular district, and in the initiation of proceedings for the collection of fines, penalties, and property forfeited to the United States as a result of illegal activities.

The Executive Office for U.S. Attorneys provides administrative support for and coordinates the activities of the 94 offices of U.S. attorneys. It is responsible for allocating personnel and budgets and managing the appointment process of all U.S. attorneys and assistant U.S. attorneys.

The Bureau of Prisons

The Bureau of Prisons is responsible for operating the entire system of federal prisons. From the moment a criminal is convicted of a federal crime and sentenced, the Bureau of Prisons is responsible for housing, feeding, and rehabilitating that person. The bureau operates all maximum, medium, and minimum security facilities and maintains contact with community programs and halfway houses that supervise convicts when they leave the prison system.

The Pardon Attorney

The Constitution authorizes the president to pardon, reduce the prison sentence of or the fine imposed upon, or grant a reprieve to any convicted criminal. This procedure is called executive clemency. Although it is rarely granted, any prisoner who wishes to be considered for executive clemency must first contact the pardon attorney within the Justice Department. After receiving such a request, the pardon attorney investigates the case, reviews the evidence, and makes a decision that is then conveyed to the attorney general. The attorney general presents that decision to the president in the form of a recommendation.

The Parole Commission

The Parole Commission is made up of a parole board and a large number of probation officers. The parole board is comprised of nine persons appointed by the president and confirmed by the Senate. They meet regularly and have the authority to grant, change, or withdraw the parole of any federal prisoner. Once a prisoner is paroled and leaves the jurisdiction of the Bureau of Prisons,

An inmate at the Mecklenburg Correctional Center in Boydton, Virginia. The Justice Department's Bureau of Prisons operates a nationwide system of maximum, medium, and minimum security prisons for those persons convicted of federal crimes.

Communications technicians of the U.S. National Central Bureau, the U.S. liaison to the International Criminal Police Organization (INTERPOL), receive incoming messages from INTERPOL member countries. INTERPOL has established a system of notices to advise all member countries about persons or property of criminal interest to the international law-enforcement community.

a probation officer takes over his or her case. Probation officers supervise parolees, making sure that they fulfill the conditions of the release set by the parole board until they are released from the system.

INTERPOL-USNCB

The International Criminal Police Organization–United States National Central Bureau (INTERPOL-USNCB) is the U.S. liaison to INTERPOL, a multinational association established in 1923 to help prevent international crime. The United States joined the organization in 1938 and continues to be a cooperating member, sharing information about crime and aiding in the capture of felons when they are on U.S. territory. Crimes of particular interest to INTERPOL include murder, robbery, narcotics sales and smuggling, counterfeiting, and international terrorism. Member nations cooperate by tracing weapons used in the commission of crimes, tracing license plates when automobiles are involved in crimes, locating and interviewing witnesses, checking the criminal records of suspected felons, and aiding in the capture of fugitives.

INTERPOL-USNCB also serves as an intermediary between law-enforcement agencies in its member countries by transmitting requests for assistance in investigations via its communications network. The attorney general serves as the U.S. representative to INTERPOL. Justice Department representatives from the FBI, U.S. Marshals Service, DEA, INS, and the Criminal Division are assigned to INTERPOL-USNCB.

Office of Justice Programs

The Office of Justice Programs helps to foster cooperation and coordination between different elements of the criminal justice system. Five offices and bureaus—the Bureau of Justice Assistance, Bureau of Justice Statistics, National Institute of Justice, Office of Juvenile Justice and Delinquency Prevention, and Office for Victims of Crime—sponsor projects to improve the U.S. criminal and juvenile justice systems through research and technical assistance.

More than 250,000 people participated in the 1963 March on Washington to promote passage of civil rights legislation. The Justice Department has placed emphasis on particular kinds of issues when the demands of society have made it necessary to do so; in the 1960s, for example, the Civil Rights Division received a large share of attention.

SIX

Justice in the Twenty-First Century

The Department of Justice today appears, at first glance, to be only dimly related to the Office of the Attorney General created in 1789 or to the small department established in 1870. Yet there is constancy and continuity in the department's steadfast commitment to fulfilling the ideals that inspired it.

Over time, priorities within society and within the department have mandated that the department place increased emphasis on particular kinds of issues. Hence, for example, during the 1960s civil rights issues and cases received a large share of attention; in the 1980s, the drug problem is a leading concern. This does not imply that the law is fickle or that the Justice Department is necessarily inconsistent in its prosecution of cases; it does indicate that the Justice Department has a responsibility to adjust both its emphasis and organizational structure to reflect the complexities of American society. In the future, as new issues and concerns emerge, they will be reflected in the structure and priorities of the Justice Department.

Many of the cases the Justice Department handles today would astound the men who helped create the department in 1870. Few Americans in the 19th century foresaw the dramatic change in attitudes that would occur by the latter half of the 20th century. American citizens no longer view the federal government as merely a governing body whose power must be guarded and

99

Two young boys share a marijuana cigarette. In the 1980s, illegal drug use is a major concern of the Justice Department.

restricted. Today, the federal government is an active player in an American society that is a partnership of the private and public sectors. People hold the federal government responsible for providing a multitude of services, as well as for the basic protection of their rights. Therefore, Justice Department lawyers handle a broad range of cases on such issues as government responsibility for toxic-waste disposal, financial liability for aircraft accidents, and the right of the federal government to exercise its immigration authority and deport Nazi war criminals who failed to disclose their past when they entered the United States.

These cases point out the special obligation of Justice Department attorneys. In 1935, in fact, the Court ruled on this issue: In *Berger* v. *United States*, the Court stated that an attorney for the United States "is the representative not of an ordinary party to a controversy, but of a sovereignty whose obligation to govern impartially is as compelling as its obligation to govern at all, and whose interest . . . is not that it shall win a case, but that justice shall be done. As such, he is in a peculiar and very definite sense, the servant of the law, the twofold aim of which is that guilt shall not escape or innocence suffer. He may prosecute with earnestness and rigor—indeed, he should do so. But, while he may strike hard blows, he is not at liberty to strike foul ones."

This definition of the obligation of an attorney for the government may appear to be at odds with the concept of a lawyer as an advocate for a particular client or position. However, it explains a great deal about the Department of Justice and the responsibility of its attorney employees. The definition explains that Justice Department lawyers represent the government and the people of the United States. More important, the definition continues, although the lawyers have a responsibility to defend the government's right to exercise power, they also have an important responsibility to guarantee that that power is exercised equitably and justly. In other words, it is central to our democratic way of life that the Justice Department represents the government and protects the rights of all citizens in courts of law. At all times, the Justice Department serves as the initial guardian of the rights of those accused of committing federal crimes because it alone has the prosecutorial discretion to initiate—or decline to initiate—a criminal investigation or prosecution. The government is also held accountable for its actions: When the government violates the law or denies rights to any citizen, the people have the right to challenge that action.

All U.S. citizens—no matter what their situation or status—have the right and capability to challenge the federal government. The Justice Department is responsible for defending its client, but that the government can lose a case and be held accountable is crucial to the preservation of democracy. This simple

The inscription *The Place of Justice is a Hallowed Place* appears on the Pennsylvania Avenue side of the Department of Justice building. It reflects the dual demand on Justice Department lawyers: to defend the government's right to exercise power and also guarantee that this power is exercised fairly, equitably, and justly.

ideal was the basis for the creation of the Office of the Attorney General in 1789 and for the expansion of that office into the Department of Justice in 1870. It remains the basis for the existence of the department today.

When visitors to Washington, D.C., walk by the Department of Justice building, they can read several inscriptions carved into the building's marble walls. One of these inscriptions reads: "No Free Government can survive that is not based on the Supremacy of the Law." This simple statement is the basis for the continuing work of the Justice Department. America's is a government of laws, not of force. Without this commitment, liberty cannot exist, and democracy cannot survive.

Department of Justice

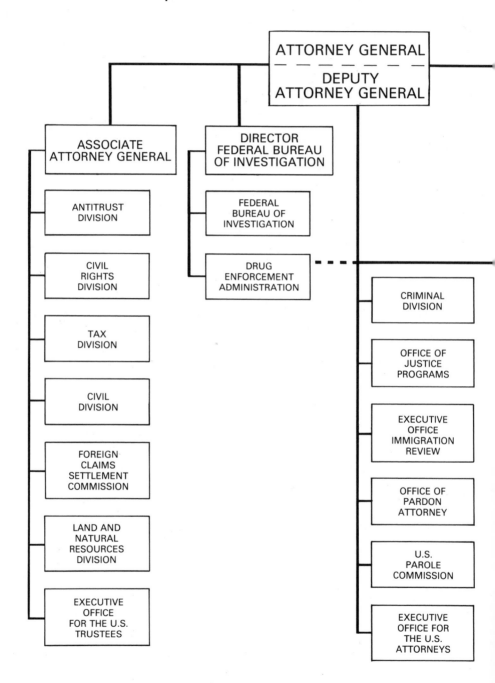

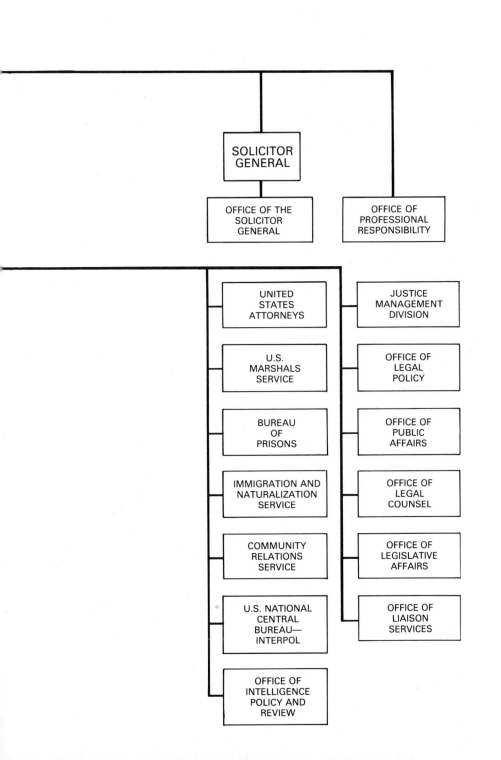

SOLICITOR
GENERAL

OFFICE OF THE
SOLICITOR
GENERAL

OFFICE OF
PROFESSIONAL
RESPONSIBILITY

UNITED
STATES
ATTORNEYS

JUSTICE
MANAGEMENT
DIVISION

U.S.
MARSHALS
SERVICE

OFFICE OF
LEGAL
POLICY

BUREAU
OF
PRISONS

OFFICE OF
PUBLIC
AFFAIRS

IMMIGRATION AND
NATURALIZATION
SERVICE

OFFICE OF
LEGAL
COUNSEL

COMMUNITY
RELATIONS
SERVICE

OFFICE OF
LEGISLATIVE
AFFAIRS

U.S. NATIONAL
CENTRAL
BUREAU—
INTERPOL

OFFICE OF
LIAISON
SERVICES

OFFICE OF
INTELLIGENCE
POLICY AND
REVIEW

GLOSSARY

Affidavit   A written declaration made under oath before a magistrate or other authorized officer.

Antitrust law   A law that regulates or prohibits unfair competition and combinations in restraint of trade, including monopolies and trusts.

Extradition   The legal process whereby an alleged criminal is surrendered by the officials of one state or country to the officials of the state or country in which the crime is alleged to have been committed.

Indictment   The formal accusation, drawn up by the prosecuting attorney and found by a grand jury, charging a person with the commission of a crime.

Litigation   Legal action; the process of prosecuting or defending by pleadings, evidence, and debate in a court.

Naturalization   The process by which people acquire citizenship in a country other than the nation of their birth.

Parole   The release of a prisoner before his term has expired on condition of continued good behavior.

Prosecuting attorney   An attorney who conducts proceedings in a court on behalf of the government. Prosecutions for the federal government are handled by U.S. attorneys.

Search warrant   A document signed by a judge that gives legal permission to search private property for stolen goods or illegal possessions.

SELECTED REFERENCES

Goddard, Donald. *Undercover: The Lives of a Federal Agent.* New York: Times Books, 1988.

Huston, Luther A. *The Department of Justice.* New York: Praeger, 1967.

Israel, Fred L. *The FBI.* New York: Chelsea House, 1986.

Navasky, Victor S. *Kennedy Justice.* New York: Atheneum, 1977.

Posner, Richard A. *The Federal Courts.* Cambridge: Harvard University Press, 1985.

Stefoff, Rebecca. *The Drug Enforcement Administration.* New York: Chelsea House, 1989.

Stewart, James B. *Prosecutors: Inside the Offices of the Government's Most Powerful Lawyers.* New York: Simon and Schuster, 1988.

Ulmer, S. Sydney, ed. *Courts, Law, and Judicial Processes.* New York: Free Press, 1981.

U.S. Department of Justice. *The Annual Report of the Attorney General of the United States, 1986.* Washington, DC: U.S. Department of Justice, 1987.

U.S. Department of Justice. *The Department of Justice . . . The Nation's Litigator.* Washington, DC: U.S. Department of Justice, 1987.

Whitehead, Don, *The FBI Story.* New York: Random House, 1956.

INDEX

Lynne Dunn is a historian in the Contemporary History Branch of the Naval Historical Center in Washington, D.C. She received an M.A. and a Ph.D. from Kent State University and has taught history at several universities, including the State University of New York at Fredonia, the University of Utah, and Miami University at Oxford, Ohio. She has contributed articles to several publications including *Women and American Foreign Policy: Critics, Lobbyists and Insiders* and *Ohio History.*

Arthur M. Schlesinger, jr., served in the White House as special assistant to Presidents Kennedy and Johnson. He is the author of numerous acclaimed works in American history and has twice been awarded the Pulitzer Prize. He taught history at Harvard College for many years and is currently Albert Schweitzer Professor of the Humanities at the City College of New York.

PICTURE CREDITS